GROWING WISER
KNOWING LESS

EMBRACING THE PARADOX OF WISDOM AND HUMILITY

MARK W. DURM

Published by Inicio Press
https://www.iniciopress.com/
Growing Wiser, Knowing Less: Embracing the Paradox of Wisdom and Humility

Print ISBN: 978-1-9992490-4-5
Ebook (epub) ISBN: 978-1-9992490-5-2

Contents

I believe that we must attack the things in which we do not believe. Not attack by the method of cutting off the heads of people, but attack in the sense of discuss. I believe that we should demand that people try in their own minds to obtain for themselves a more consistent picture of their own world; that they not permit themselves the luxury of having their brain cut in four pieces or two pieces even, and on one side they believe this, and on the other side they believe that, but never try to compare the two points of view. Because we have learned that by trying to put the points of view that we have in our head together and comparing one to the other, we make some progress in understanding and in appreciating where we are and what we are.

~Richard Feynman

Dedication

I dedicate this to my deceased parents, Darwin and Odell Durm, who gave me life, and to my three children, Spencer, Sydni, and Sophi, who have made that life interesting and fulfilling.

Acknowledgments

This publication is the product of many people. The staff of the *Athens News Courier* collectively and Kelly Kazek especially were instrumental in initiating and continuing these essays. At the beginning of 2003, I asked Kelly Kazek if I could submit materials for columns to be included in the Sunday newspaper. She agreed and encouraged me throughout the process.

I commend Celeste Bedingfield, Debbi Kelley, and Nancy Morgan for deciphering my handwriting. In the 16-year span over which the essays were published, these women assisted me in ways that went above and beyond the call of duty. They deserve ribbons for their work on my behalf.

Kenneth Collins, Tracy Hicks, and Jesse Hudgins of the Athens State University Printing Services also deserve recognition.

I am grateful to Linda Tucker, my editor at Cup and Quill Editing and Publication Services, LLC. Her professionalism and expertise were instrumental in moving this project to publication. I also thank the entire staff at Cup and Quill for their encouragement and assistance.

Finally, I acknowledge Spencer, Sydni, and Sophi, my three children, for their patience and encouragement.

To each and all, I could not have done it without you.

Importantly, any errors or mistakes are due to me and not any of the people listed above.

Foreword

This book consists of ninety-six newspaper columns written over sixteen years, from 2003 to 2019. They primarily appeared in the Sunday edition of the *Athens News Courier*, Athens, Alabama. When one writes, the results usually fall into one of two categories. You can write statements that align with what most people already believe. Such statements make people feel warm, fuzzy, and comfortable. However, such writing changes little, if anything, about how or what they think.

Or you can write to afflict the comfortable, to stir up their minds, and make those brain cells get a little exercise. I prefer the stirring; maybe that is related to being a college professor for forty-five years. I always loved looking into my students' eyes and seeing the light bulbs switching on between their ears.

The mind is like a rubber band; it can never return to its original size once you stretch it. So, I love stirring, switching, and stretching! So as you read these articles, my hope is to afflict you.

These essays are about life. Due to teaching critical thinking at the university level for many years, many focus on critical thinking or the lack thereof.

There are three columns on "Truth Fragments," one of which concerns church burnings and female breast cancer—no, they are not related except in relation to misguided thinking.

There are two on the "Stubbornness Of Misinformation," two on "Beware Of Big Numbers, Usually A Bunch Of Bull," two on "Cause And Effect: On Growing Wiser and Knowing Less," "Ignorance About Medicine Risks And Dying," "Admitting We Know Less about More," "Your World View and Stretching Rubber Bands," and several others.

Several are about family: "Is America Becoming A Matriarchal Society," "Family Values," "Understanding The Stopped Watch Syndrome," "Where Have All The Fathers Gone," "Children's Bodies Growing Adult At Earlier Ages," "The Biggest, Strongest Man I Know," "Then I Have A Very Good Mother," and others.

Several are about religion: three columns on the "Foundations Of Easter," "Was Jesus 43 When He Died?'; "What Is The Color Of God?," "When Does Behavior Become A Sin?," "A Story About God And Tornadoes," "Why

Isn't Christmas On March 25th," "Religions Should Unite People Not Divide Them," and others.

Some of my more controversial essays, judged from the community's response, combined religion and critical thinking. There are three entitled "Evolution, Is It The Handiwork Of God," "It Was Just His Time To Go-It's Easier To Believe In Fate," "Man Deserves Some Credit, Not Just God," and "Misunderstandings All In The Translation," "Better To Be Ready Than Proverbial," "An Admitted Wrong As Compared To An Amended Wrong," and others.

Some essays are centered around politics. Two of my favorite ones are entitled "America Needs More Purple People" and "Cut Taxes-Where Do We Cut Spending?". Others are "The Wall Between Church And State Should Stand," "Do We Really Live In A Democracy," and others.

Finally, "the Society of America" has its essays also. One is about "Guns," another is entitled "Patriotism And The Type Of War," others include "Many Owe Health To Cancer Victims" (the victim was Henrietta Lacks, an African American lady); "The God Of Credit," "Maggots, Mortgage Loans, Dog Poop, And A Dodge Truck," there are two articles on the "History Of Abortion," and others.

Readers can read the essays in whatever order they prefer based on what catches their interest in the Table of Contents. May you stir, switch, and stretch to your heart's and mind's content. Perhaps you'll discover, as I did, that the more you learn, the less you know. I invite you to embrace the journey toward growing wiser and knowing less.

Religions Should Unite People, Not Divide Them'
Part 1 of 2

Article #1
The News Courier, February 9, 2003

Approximately two billion Christians and one to two billion Muslims live in this world. Neither side will be able to convert the other. They must learn to have mutual respect and acceptance. They must, as Jesus said, treat others as they want to be treated—the Golden Rule (Matthew 7:12). They must, as the Koran reads, be expected to give full measure if they wish to receive full measure (83:1). That is their "Golden Rule."

The Koran acknowledges Jesus. He is mentioned approximately twenty-five times in the Koran.

The Muslims do not believe he was the Son of God, but they do praise him greatly. For instance, his birth (3:45-47; 19:22-33), his message and miracles (5:110; 19:30-33), his righteousness as a prophet (6:85), the compassion and mercy of his followers (57:27), and many more aspects of his life are told.

Christians, on the other hand, know very little, if anything, about Muhammad. Moreover, very few Christians have read or even looked at the Koran. They should.

Religions should unite people, not divide them. Life is sacred to Islam and Christianity (Koran 17:33; Matthew 19:14), and both highly value forgiveness (Koran 42:37; Matthew 9:2).

The agreements between the Bible and the Koran are many. The two religions must emphasize their commonalities and not their differences.

The Koran in 2:62 reads:

> *Those who believe (in the Koran). And those who follow the Jewish (scripture)*
> *And the Christians and the Sabians.*
> *Any who believe in Allah*
> *And the Last Day*
> *And work righteousness,*
> *Shall have their reward*
> *With their Lord on them*

Shall be no fear, nor shall they grieve.

These verses from the Koran reveal that Islam recognizes other religions.

As a matter of fact, in 5:82-85, the Koran says Christians are nearest in love to Islam.

My great-grandmother, Nannie Spencer Snell, had a religious philosophy that would benefit the world. If she learned that an individual had different religious views, she would respond, "Well, that is him and his God." She said this with love, respect, and acceptance. She said this because of the peace she had in her heart. She knew that peace between family members and nations comes from acceptance.

My great-grandmother believed very strongly in Matthew 5:9, which reads, "Blessed are the peacemakers: for they shall be called the children of God."

The Koran offers in 8:61, "But if the enemy incline toward peace do thou (also) incline toward peace...."

We Can All Learn From 'Peace be still'
Part 2 of 2

Article #2
The News Courier, February 16, 2003

Religions should work together for peace. Peace will come through acceptance of each other.

Muslims are even instructed to live in peace with non-believers. The Koran in 60:8-9 reads as follows:

Allah forbids you not, with regard to those who Fight you not for (your) Faith... From dealing kindly and justly with them: For Allah loveth Those who are just.
Allah only forbids you.
With regard to those who (do)
Fight you for (your) Faith
From turning to them
(For friendship and protection).
It is such as turn to them
(In these circumstances), That
do wrong.

The above verses instruct Muslims to deal kindly and justly with non-believers in the Muslim faith unless they are out to destroy it. These verses from the Koran should cause Christians to question their proselytizing of Muslims.

If the Muslim people are happy with their religion, why does the Christian faith send missionaries to some of these areas?

One can witness the recent deaths of Christian missionaries in Yemen and Lebanon. In Lebanon, three Baptist missionaries were killed in December 2002.

In November of 2002, an American missionary nurse was shot to death in Lebanon, where local Muslim clerics objected to proselytizing by foreign Christians.

The approach by many Christians who evangelize is to work formally in a secular field and to proselytize informally.

Believe it or not, this method is criticized greatly by some Christian humanitarians who work in these areas. For example, a top official of the Hungarian Interchurch Aid Office feels this informal approach is deceptive and causes Muslims to vent their anger toward all Christian aid workers.

Would not many who believe in Christianity be upset if a Muslim tried to convert them? The Christian faith should live by its own Golden Rule.

Again, in Matthew 7:12, Jesus said, "in everything, do unto others what you would have them do unto you."

It seems "everything" would cover proselytizing.

If the Christians do not want to be proselytized by the Muslims, they should not proselytize them.

The fanatical Christian conservatives may do more harm than good. They preach that the Muslim faith is violent and evil.

From the Muslim perspective, the fanatical Muslim clerics who preach jihad do more harm than good.

The fanatics in both religions are escalating the discord.

The moderates in both faiths must calm the disturbance, and they both must shout *Peace be still*.

Peace between the two religions may develop if the moderates become more active and accountable.

Minds mimic rivers. That is, where rivers are most shallow, they make the most noise; where they are the deepest, they are the quietest.

The Christian and Muslim worlds can ill afford to imitate rivers; no longer should the most shallow minds make the most noise.

Saner voices must become louder! Oddly, peace and stillness may only occur through the loudness of moderation.

In the Bible, Ecclesiastes 3:7 reads, "there is a time to keep silent and a time to speak." Voices of moderation need to speak; it is time!

Hopefully, Christianity and Islam shall find peace and cooperation.

Just think what could be accomplished by 3.2 billion people were united and not divided.

"Peace, be still."

No Child Left Behind—Impossible!

Article #3
The News Courier, March 16, 2003

As an educator with thirty years of experience, I get rather frustrated that society believes that the educational system can and should correct all the ills of our society. It cannot, and it never will. It may correct some, but not all. Schools can reduce ignorance, but they can never alleviate it.

President Bush's "No child left behind" law makes a good political sound bite, but it is light on reality. There will always be children left behind. Those children left behind will be of two types—one of *nature* and one of *nurture*. The one of nature is the child who does not have the raw intellect to stay up, that is, the child whose intelligence is one standard deviation below the mean. (Note: I am speaking of *intelligence*, not *intelligence quotient*; there is a big difference.) These children make up approximately 16 percent of all children.

The second child is the one whose environment *outside* school is not conducive to learning. This is due to the 9/91 factor. That is, between one's birth and their nineteenth birthday, a child will spend 9 percent of his time in school and 91 percent outside of it. Today's teachers do well to control the 9 percent, much less the 91 percent.

Of those variables that cause performance differences among schools, an official in the Educational Testing Service (ETS) estimated that approximately 90 percent is due to things the teacher has little control over. Those variables include the number of hours spent watching television, the kind and amount of reading material in the students' homes, the number of days students are absent from class, and the number of pages pupils read for homework (note, it states *read* not *assigned*; the teacher can assign it, but it may not be read), and finally, and this may be the most relevant, the *number of parents* in the home.

I argue that those who control 91 percent of students' time, not those who control the 9 percent, leave behind more children.

It is easy to blame teachers. Ignorance searches for the easiest solution, not the correct one. If schools fail, blame the teachers. If athletic teams fail, blame the coaches. I wonder if Bush's No Child Left Behind Act includes sports. If 100 students sign up to play a varsity sport, do they all get to suit up and play? I think not. But this is exactly what is expected of teachers. All 100 students are expected to play the game of life, be productive, and not be left behind.

And as I said before, ignorance searches for the easiest answer, not the correct one. The amount of money (taxes) spent per child has no relationship to that child's academic performance. Spending more money is the easy answer; it is not the correct one (I will write more about that later).

Thus, children will always be left behind. The ones left behind due to 'nature' are outside our control. The ones left behind due to 'nurture' are in the parents' control. If taxes were increased to aid in children's academic performance, the money might be well spent on family and marriage counselors.

The Gulf War: An Illusion of Certainty

Article #4
The News Courier, April 20, 2003

We all like to be certain about life. The human mind likes "certainty." It can create it where there is none.

For instance, look at the two tables in the figure, which Roger Shepard designed in 1990.

The table on the left looks "certainly" narrower and longer than the wider one on the right. It's not! The two tables are the same size.

If you don't believe me (and you don't), take a piece of thin paper and trace the outline of the table on the left, then hold the outline over the table on the right.

Alas, they are the same! You will "measure" that they are the same, but you will not "see" that they are. Your brain will not let you.

Your perceptual system creates a "certain" impression from uncertain cues. This is called the "illusion of certainty."

In my Critical Thinking class at Athens State University, I teach that we should always be on guard against this illusion when we interpret the world around us. Thus, I claim, "The more you know, the less you know you know!"

I have written all that to write this; the war in Iraq is filled with uncertainty, howbeit, there are two sides, and both sides are "certain" they are right.

Their brains, and thus their minds, will not let them see it any other way.

Their collective minds have created a "certain" impression from uncertain cues.

This Gulf war is different from the first one in many ways and in one way in particular—the media.

Let me add here, if I may, that I currently have the pleasure of being a college professor and have the past honor of being a decorated veteran of the first Gulf war. Thus, I have some experience related to what I write.

During the first Gulf war in 1991, only CNN recorded it in real-time for those who watched it worldwide.

Moreover, very few Arab homes then had the equipment to receive it. Not so this time.

For the present conflict, twelve Arab television networks compete daily for the Middle East viewer. What they see is not what we see. They create a "certain" impression from uncertain cues, just as we do.

They know for "certain" that this war reinforces their beliefs about the hypocrisy of the United States and its Middle Eastern policy and philosophy.

The suicide bombers are called "martyrs" on Arab television, the "war in Iraq" they label as the "war on Iraq," and the conflict is termed jihad, the holy war.

In contrast, we are "certain" that the Middle East would like to be like us and would do and be better if they adopted our forms of government and lifestyles.

We, too, suffer from the illusion of certainty.

From time to time during this war, I watched the Canadian Broadcasting Corporation's coverage on C-SPAN.

It is a different conflict from the one I watch on the American broadcasting systems. My illusion of certainty is challenged.

But the greatest challenge the Arabs and we face may not be this war but what occurs after the war.

We must shed our illusions of certainty about each other and learn to work and live with each other.

Both sides must come to the discussion table with open minds because both tables in this discussion are the same size.

A Story About God and Tornadoes

Article #5
The News Courier, May 11, 2003

God and tornadoes, John Doe and Jim Smith, a mattress and a nail, hogs eating dead flesh, and my maternal great-aunt, Mrs. Avalene, are related topics in this column. Let us begin.

Often after a destructive tornado, you and I have heard people exclaim on television that God "spared" them and their property. That may be so—I do not claim to speak for God. However, in my opinion, the omnipotence of God, as told by the Bible, and tornadoes that destroy life and property make strange bedfellows.

When I hear that statement, the next scene on tv is often a neighbor whose property was destroyed, and they may have lost a loved one. If God "spared" the first man but not the second, what is the second man to think? Is he to believe God allowed his family to die and destroyed his property?

Let me develop my scenario using John Doe and Jim Smith, fictional characters based on a true story concerning my great-aunt Mrs. Avalene.

Let us say that a tornado has struck Main Street in Anytown, USA. On this street live two men who are adjacent neighbors. John Doe and his family live in House A, and Jim Smith and his family live in House B.

John Doe's family and house are spared. No damage at all. John Doe loudly exclaims that God blessed him. Within earshot, however, is Jim Smith, and he has just lost his wife and one child to the tornado. He has another son who is injured badly and in a coma. His other children are spared. His house and belongings, however, are destroyed. Jim, in total despair, hears John loudly and proudly exclaiming to God and giving thanks. Hanging his head, Jim asks, "If God is all-powerful, did He not want to spare my family?"

Continuing the scenario, Jim Smith and his family were much more virtuous than John Doe. John Doe occasionally cheated on his taxes and his wife. Jim Smith never did.

Here is the true story of Mrs. Avalene, my great-aunt, as told to me by my grandmother. In 1952 a tornado struck a house in a valley in Franklin County, TN. My great-uncle Clifton, his wife Avalene, and their six children lived in this house. The children ranged from Bobby, age eleven, to Gail, a one-month-old baby. Uncle Clifton was a farmer.

The tornado struck early in the night. It picked up their house and spewed it in all directions. One side of the house fell on my uncle, pinning him to the ground. All was chaos. My aunt clutched the baby and sat close to her pinned husband. A few feet from her was her son, Doyle. He was dead. Bobby, the oldest boy, had a nail driven into his head and lay unconscious in the dark night. He would live but remain in a coma for many days. Linda, the youngest girl, could not be found either. The next morning, she would be found unhurt, wrapped in a mattress in a tree.

During the night, Mrs. Avalene sent Jimmy, the second oldest boy, about age nine, to climb the hillside, go to the ridge, and seek help. Jimmy never reached the top. He was found asleep the next morning on the hillside.

He was probably in shock. Not hearing from Jimmy, my great-aunt sent Robbie, the oldest girl. Early the next morning, Robbie reached the top and found help.

Something more chilling happened during the darkness of the night. My great-uncle, Clifton, remained pinned but alive. Remember, neither he nor Avalene knew the whereabouts of all their children; some were missing. Clifton heard bones popping and flesh being eaten. He thought his hogs were eating his children. (The hogs were eating the dead chickens.) He struggled to get up. He died. Mrs. Avalene sat through the long dark night with her dead husband, one dead child, and her one-month-old baby cuddled in her arms. The night was long. Clifton and Avalene were some of the most virtuous people in the community.

In the following years, Mrs. Avalene raised her family by herself. She worked in a factory to feed and clothe her remaining five children. She never remarried nor dated again. She and some other Jim Smiths of the world have a lot in common.

Some readers will give the "Job" answer to Mrs. Avalene's predicament. In the Old Testament, Job lost his seven sons and three daughters to a "great wind." But, Job 42:12-14 reads: "So the Lord blessed Job at the end of his life more than at the beginning.... God also gave him seven more sons and three more daughters."

Not so for Mrs. Avalene. As I write this, she sits alone in a small wooden frame house on the outskirts of Winchester, TN. She has only two children left. Bobby, the eldest boy, died of cancer in his early adult life. Robbie, the eldest daughter, died of cancer in early adulthood. Gail, the one-month-old baby boy, drowned at age sixteen in 1968. Jimmy, her only surviving son, has brain cancer, and Linda, the girl on the mattress, is her only surviving daughter. Mrs. Avalene has had a severe stroke. Sadly, she may live long enough to bury all her children.

She sits alone in her house, as do other Jim Smiths of the world in their houses. God and tornadoes—I do not understand the connection.

John Doe does.

A Father's Day Special
How one man discovered the fountain of youth

Article #6

The News Courier, June 2003

I have discovered the fountain of youth. It is my son, Spencer, who is three. I am fifty-three.

I live in a world of half-eaten cereal bars, fully scattered toys, lost sippy cups, and five-minute bubble gum. I have rediscovered frogs, turtles, bugs, and kittens. I love every minute of it.

Spencer has introduced me to an amazing colorful menagerie. There is this huge purple dinosaur named Barney; Clifford, a big red dog; Pooh, a mid-size yellow bear that lives in a 100-acre wood; a pint-sized pink pig named Piglet; and an orange and black bouncing tiger named Tigger.

I know who Peanut, Butter, and Jelly Otter are. I know that "Wiggles" is a noun, not a verb. Also, I am acquainted with Sponge Bob, Rolie Polie Olie, Lloyd in Space, and Jay the Jet Plane.

When most men my age go to auditoriums to listen to rock-and-roll singers of the past or see country music stars, I see the future with Bob the Builder and his if "can we fix it" genera-tion. I love every minute of it.

Each morning I am awakened by Spen-cer's one-word wake-up call—"Da-addy"—from his bedroom. As I pick him up and give him his first hug of the day, he lays his head on my shoulder and greets me with the same sleepy salutation— "I want some chocolate milk," followed by "a whole bunch."

During Spencer's three years, I have learned much about my world. He has shown me how to find the only mud pud-dle in any five-acre field and dip water with a shoe. Once when we stopped at a service station, I told him that we were going to get a little gas. He replied, "Daddy, can we stop and get some big gas?"

Spencer has to live in my world; I love living in his. The other morning, he fed me breakfast. He offered a menu of potatoes, a large piece of pizza, and cake. My older eyes saw a small green plastic turtle–the potato, a coat hanger–the pizza, and a little lime-green walrus–the cake. I enjoyed the meal.

After breakfast, we flew in a plane with him sitting on my lap. We winged our way to Tennessee to see Nanny and Pa Durm and then to Oklahoma to visit Meemaw and Peepaw Wells.

On our long adventurous trip, we viewed the tops of fluffy white clouds and never left the bedroom floor.

In Spencer's world, "Fifty dollars" consists of a quarter, one dime, and three pennies. Oh, I wish it were so.

I have been blessed in my fifty-three years—life has been much better than I deserve. I have received a few awards, but none better than the one I received on Saturday morning, May 24, 2003. After Spencer's wake-up call and perfunctory chocolate milk, he lay in bed with me, his little head perched on my arm after gently covering him. We watched Disney's cassette tape of "Aristocats" for the twenty-third time. Then he turned to me and said softly, "Daddy, thank you for you."

At that moment, I felt ten feet tall.

Yes, I have found the fountain of youth. It is a three-year-old, blond-haired, and blue-eyed ball of energy.

Because of him, I exercise better, eat healthier, and laugh longer. I do not jog anymore; I chase. Also, I smile on the inside a lot more. Smiling on the inside is healthy for the heart and the soul. I love this ball of energy "a whole bunch." He favors his mother, Tracy, and not me—thank goodness.

I pray that when he is thirteen and twenty-three, he will still stand beside me, turn gently, and say softly, "Dad, thank you for you."

The Dilemma of Earlier Physical Development

Article #7
The New Courier, July 30, 2003

In AD 2100, an eight-year-old girl will become a mother.

Yes, in less than 100 years, eight-year-old females will become mothers. Impossible? In 1998, the youngest mother in Alabama was eleven years old. From 1999 to 2001, the youngest mother in Alabama was twelve.

Teenagers are children in adult bodies. This phenomenon of earlier physical development is known as the "secular trend." This trend is occurring in parts of the world with high living standards.

Our children enter puberty increasingly earlier, at four months per decade. Thus, the girl in 1998 who became a mother at eleven will have a compatriot in 2098 who will be eight. As for boys, they also follow this trend. The youngest father in Alabama in 1998 was 13. In 1999, 2000, and 2002, the youngest father in this state was 14.

Some think in the "olden days," women were younger when they had children compared to today. They couldn't; they hadn't even started menarche, the beginning of menstruation. The Scandinavian countries, which keep the best medical records in the world, have been documenting this phenomenon for 160 years. In Norway, in the 1840s, the average age of menarche was seventeen; by the 1970s, it was slightly above age thirteen. In Finland, the average age in 1860 was sixteen and one-half; by 1970, it had dropped to thirteen.

The United States started keeping records in approximately 1905. The average age for menarche then was just above fourteen; by 1965, it had dropped to around twelve years, eight months. Dr. Michael Freemark, Chief of Pediatric Endocrinology at Duke University Medical Center in Durham, North Carolina, says they frequently encounter young girls between five to ten with breasts or pubic hair.

What about boys? They, too, are maturing at a younger age. Boys are becoming men physically and sexually earlier, but emotionally they are still boys. When I played football in high school in the 1960s, we had one of the largest lines in Tennessee, averaging 200 pounds. In football today, a line that averaged 200 pounds would be pushed all over the field. High school lines now average 250 pounds or more. I once remarked to my Adolescent Psychology class at Athens State University that someday a high school football player would weigh 400 pounds. Well, "someday" has already occurred.

What is causing this alarming situation? The answer is probably related to nutrition. Teenagers eat higher protein and fatty diets. They gain weight quicker, mature earlier, and have sex younger. It is probably not food additives, as some might think. There were no food additives in the 1800s in the Scandinavian countries. I read that since the introduction of fast-food hamburgers in Japan, the average Japanese teenager has gained ten pounds.

I believe the brain's hypothalamus, our "thermostat," if one pleases, is involved. I believe it is genetically coded that when each individual reaches a certain weight, it "thermostatically" starts the hormones flowing, inducing secondary sex characteristics, thus pubescence. That weight occurs earlier and earlier due to diet.

I also believe genes have a lower age limit for pubescence. That is, I think there is a minimum age at which it will not allow pubescence to occur. But I fear it is several years younger than eleven. In 2098, we may have an eight-year-old mother.

The secular trend is a dilemma. A solution will not come easily and, I fear, will exact a huge price on young people. It already has. Eleven and twelve-year-old girls are too young to be mothers. Thirteen and fourteen-year-old boys are not ready for fatherhood.

I Pay Eighty-seven Cents an Acre and $836 for One-Third Acre

Article #8
The New Courier, August 17, 2003

Yes, the above is true on property tax, so do I favor Gov. Riley's tax proposal? Both sides are promoting propaganda. I have likes and dislikes.

Mainly I dislike that none of the proposed tax increases are earmarked for anything, especially education. Instead, the increases go into an account entitled "excellence fund." There are other wrinkles in the tax proposal that I dislike. One is that the sixteen private sector utilities are not having their taxes increased. Another wrinkle is that most property taxes, except for Section 8 rental properties, will increase. Section 8 properties are rental units where the federal government mostly pays the rent. The exception exists because two powerful state legislators own Section 8 properties. This is a cowardly shame by those who should lead.

Although I own rental houses, I do not "cotton" to Section 8 rental properties. I have one rental house in Athens that sits on a one-third acre plot. I paid $836 in property taxes on it last year. For another rental house, I paid $503. At the same time, I have a thirty-one-acre plot of ground that borders the city limits. I have been paying $27 annually for the entire plot. Yes, that is right, I paid eighty-seven cents an acre in property tax in 2002. I also have a 100-acre plot that borders this property, and last year, I paid $1.21 per acre in tax for this property.

I was raised on a farm. I have fed cattle in the bone-chilling cold of the frigid winter and hung tobacco in a tin-roofed barn in the hot, humid summers. As a teenager, I carried a newborn calf in the snow and ice from a hollow to the warmth of the wood stove in my mother's kitchen to give it a chance at life. As a small boy, I was almost overcome by heat while chopping thistles with a hoe. My fellow farmers, eighty-seven cents an acre compared to $836 for a house and one-third an acre is not fair. You know it, and I know it.

Some of you who know me will say, "Sure, he is for the tax increase; he is a college professor." Let me address this issue.

Yes, I am a teacher and proud of it. My mother had a tenth-grade education, and my father has twelfth-grade. I did not have an indoor commode until I was in the sixth grade, and I did not own a car with air conditioning until after I had my doctorate. I have never owned a new vehicle in my entire life. I put myself through college and graduate school. I ate so much cheap soup in college that I still have a distaste for it. Yes, I teach. I know what a good education can add and have seen what a poor education can subtract. My education afforded me an opportunity, and I have tried to make the best of it.

My parents gave me something better than money; they taught me the value of it. During my adult life, not only have I worked full-time, but I have done additional part-time jobs. For a few years, I worked one full-time and three part-time jobs. Over twelve years, I worked one full-time and two part-time jobs. I write this not to boast but because I live in America.

Because of these extra jobs, I have paid more taxes. Some argue that "we already pay enough in taxes." Well, those people are right! We pay enough to be ranked forty-seventh in state and local government expenditures for elementary and secondary education. We pay enough to be ranked forty-eighth in the high school graduation rate. Also, we pay enough to be ranked forty-third in total taxes paid per person.

Some also argue that the state government should cut all the waste before we raise taxes. I agree, but let us think logically for a moment. Do you not think that a Republican governor would do everything in his power not to raise taxes? In my opinion, Governor Riley has done just that. He cut almost one-quarter of a billion dollars in state spending before he proposed the tax referendum. There seems to be nothing else to cut without jeopardizing state services in needed areas.

I agree that there is waste among state agencies, organizations, and schools. But most people forget that state entities cannot run as "mean and lean" as private corporations. One reason is that state-run entities are covered by federal laws, requirements, and mandates. Private corporations could not be as mean and lean if they had to abide by these same federal laws.

I estimate that if the tax referendum passes, I will pay close to an additional $3,000 just in property taxes alone, largely due to my rental holdings. But I will gladly pay if it causes Alabama to lead the nation and not follow it like a whipped puppy. Again, my parents taught me the value of money; it is meant to be saved and should also be invested.

If the referendum passes, I do not think there should be any salary increases for state workers, me included, for the next several years. It is senseless and not good stewardship to raise state taxes and give everyone in the state a raise. If the tax proposal passes, I believe that it can be the door that opens many possibilities for Alabama and her future. If it fails, I fear Alabama will become the doormat of the nation and the South.

I did not vote for Governor Riley in 2002, but if he runs again, I sure will. Like no other Alabama governor I have ever known, Governor Riley has stepped up to the plate. Let us collectively throw him the ball by voting for this referendum. Future Alabamians and we will benefit.

Misunderstandings All in the Translation

Article #9
The New Courier, November 2, 2003

Moses Statue

For centuries Christians believed Jewish people had horns! For approximately two thousand years, rich people have been told they will have a difficult road to heaven. And in Taiwan, Pepsi-Cola has been advertised as a miracle drink because it could bring their ancestors back from the dead! What do all of these have in common? Mistranslation from one language to another.

Mistranslating from one language to another is becoming more serious. Several of the main players in the twenty-first century have languages that come from different families. Thus, confusion and mistranslation abound and are more apt to occur. Just ask the American soldier in Iraq. But let me first return to horns, camels, and Pepsi-Cola.

For centuries in the Middle Ages, Christians believed Jews had horns. Why? Blame it partly on Michelangelo. Michelangelo's famous statue of the biblical Moses has horns. Why on earth would this famous sculptor chisel horns on one of the most beloved Old Testament characters?

The Hebrew word "Karan," which means 'ray of light' was mistranslated into Greek in the second century as "keren," which defines "horns." Thus Michelangelo believed Moses had horns, as did multitudes of Christians. It has been written that when the Crusaders reached the Holy Lands in the Middle Ages, they were astonished to find that Jews did not have the pointed things coming from their heads.

As for rich people and heaven, most church-goers have heard sermons based on Matthew 19:24: "It is easier for a camel to go through the eye of the needle than for a rich man to enter the Kingdom of Heaven." Everyone knows it is physically impossible for a camel to go through such a small opening. But this saying is due to a mistranslation, I believe. Jesus spoke Aramaic, an eastern language. The authorized Bible of the Christian Church of the East is the Peshitta. Again, the Peshitta uses language much closer to the language Jesus used. Matthew 19:24 in the Peshitta reads, "It is easier for a rope to go through the eye of a needle...." This is probably the analogy Jesus intended. It makes much more sense. As for the tunnel, "the eye of the needle" in the Holy Lands that camels must crawl through was a much later tradition to the best of my knowledge. Thus, for rich people, there is no hope.

And now to Pepsi-Cola and its "risen dead" belief. In Taiwan. The famous soft drink slogan "Come alive with the Pepsi generation" was translated as "Pepsi will bring your ancestors back from the dead!"

Other comedic mistranslations include Kentucky Fried Chicken's slogan of "Finger Lickin Good," which became "Eat your fingers off" in China. In Brazil, the Ford Pinto flopped. "Pinto" is Brazilian slang for "tiny male genitals."

In Barcelona, a hospital sign in English reads, "Visitors: two to a bed and half an hour only." There are countless humorous mistranslations, but I now want to return to the seriousness of mistranslations and our soldiers in Iraq.

The written languages of the Iraqis and the Arab world do not use letters. They use 'inscriptive drawings.'

A constant problem one hears from the American soldier in Iraq is communicating with the native people. Mistranslations will be numerous. Americans use letters; Iraqis do not.

I hope no horns, camels, or a Pepsi will affect the bargaining table or the peace agreement. Language miscommunication can cause the loss of life.

Why Isn't Christmas on March 25?

Article #10
The News Courier, December 21, 2003

Why isn't Christmas on March 25? Well, it used to be, so to speak. But keeping time has not always been an exact science. It is highly unlikely that Jesus was born on December 25 or March 25. No one really knows the precise day of his birth. We celebrate his birth on December 25 due to pagan influence. Let us delve into this matter.

"Saturnalia" was the major festival of the year in ancient Rome. It occurred around the winter solstice (literally, "the sun stands still.") When the Julian calendar (named after Julius Caesar) was first used, the solstice fell on December 21. The Julian calendar, however, was not exactly accurate. It had an error of eleven minutes per year, so by the third century AD, the solstice had moved forward to December 24.

During the third century, the emperor Aurelian established holidays on December 24 and 25 called "Sol Invicti." Sol Invicti means "unconquered sun," and the holiday honored the Syrian god, "Sol," and Aurelian himself. The emperors were thought to be the divine incarnation of Apollo. This holiday declaration basically established December 25 as the official solstice. All other sun god religions accepted December 25 as their celebration date.

The earliest Christians celebrated Jesus's birth and resurrection on the same day, March 25. March 25 was assumed to be the vernal equinox (literally equal night and day, twelve hours night, and twelve hours day). Today the equinox occurs on March 22. (Remember that the eleven-minute error had pushed everything forward by about three days).

Later, Christians celebrated the birth of Christ on January 6. One of the festivals for the Egyptian Earth mother goddess, Isis, influenced this date.

By the fourth century, many Christians referred to December 25 as the day of the "unconquered SON," not SUN, in defiance of the emperor. Also, the Christians called January 6 "Epiphany" (the coming of the magi, the baptism of Christ, or maybe even both).

In AD 350, Pope Julius I officially decreed that the birth of Christ was to be celebrated on December 25, the same day as all other sun gods.

Many churches, however, did not want to associate with pagan religions. So to this day, the Eastern Orthodox Christian Church celebrates the birth of Christ on January 7, one day after Epiphany; thus, our "Twelve days of Christmas" song, from December 25 to January 6. Its origin starts with a sun god and ends with an Earth mother goddess.

And oh, by the way, the eleven-minute error was corrected in AD 1582 by Pope Gregory. By this time, the Julian calendar had caused a ten-day error, and things were sometimes chaotic.

So today, we operate on the Gregorian calendar – and the rest, as they say, is history.

I would like to wish everyone a very merry Christmas. It is my favorite time of the year.

Do We Really Live in A Democracy?

Article #11
The New Courier, January 25, 2004

Do we really live in a democracy? Not when it comes to choosing a president of the United States. It is the season to start this process again, and it is fraught with inequities.

Every four years during this process by the political parties, I am reminded of the book by George Orwell entitled "Animal Farm." When the farm animals had overthrown the farmers, they thought there would be equality among them. A sign on the barn even read, "All animals are created equal." But one day in the barnyard, the animals looked up and noticed something had been added to the sign. It now read, "All animals are created equal, but some are more equal than others." A few select animals, the pigs, had taken over the farmhouse and were now "in charge." We, in Alabama, live in an Orwellian world regarding politics.

Democracy is defined as a form of government in which the will of the majority prevails, in which there is equality, and in which decisions are made to maximize the common good. Are these guidelines true for the United States? Not in presidential politics because some are more equal than others.

To begin with, if the will of the voting majority prevailed, Albert Gore would now be president. In 2000, he beat George Bush by 500,000 votes, but George Bush became president. Why? Because of something called an Electoral College. Why an Electoral College? Because at the Constitution Convention in 1787, the delegates did not think the common man was smart enough or educated enough to elect a president. Again, some men are created more equal than others.

As for input into the presidential selection process, Alabama has none. Iowa does. New Hampshire does. Some states are more equal than others. This does not say much for democracy's "equality," does it?

As for decisions in a democracy to maximize the common good, I do not think this happens in America. However, what is common is that decisions are made in favor of those with the most money.

We have become a government of special interest groups, political action committees, and rich people's pockets. To be elected, one must have money or have someone else's money.

In 2000, the campaign for Congress and the presidency cost $3.5 billion, up from $2.2 billion in 1996. The median expenditure on a Senate race in 2000 was $4 million. Poor people need not apply; they are less equal.

In America, one hears that any child can become president. Let's see. All have been men, all have been white, and most have been wealthy. Not just any child, because some children are more equal than others.

Therefore, in the November presidential general election of 2004, I will probably have to choose between two, and only two, white men into whose candidacy I had no input at all. If I do not give any money to either party, I will probably have very little, if any, influence. And If I vote for the one who receives the most votes, he may still not be president.

Ah, living in a democracy—there is nothing like it when selecting our president.

New York Is Much Safer Than Alabama

Article #12
The New Courier, February 8, 2004

Occasionally I hear someone ask, "Who in their right mind would want to live in New York with all of its crimes, murders, burglaries, and road fatalities?"

Let me live in the South, where it is so much safer. Is the South safer? I am afraid not. The state of New York is overall much safer than the state of Alabama.

I write this article not to discourage those who live in the South but to encourage us to do better; I am as Southern as you can get; listen to my accent. I have lived half my life in Alabama, the other half in Tennessee, and I have been educated in four Southern states.

But let us return to the matter at hand. Our belief that Alabama is much safer than New York is, like so many other erroneous beliefs, due to the misinterpretation of data. Yes, New York has almost three times the number of crimes as Alabama, but New York has over four times our state's population. Thus, one should study the crime rate per 100,000 population and not the simple total number of crimes.

Using this as our methodological guide and the most recent National Uniform Crime Report as our data, Alabama has more crime than New York. That is, on several indices used to measure the crime rate, Alabama is a much less safe place to live than our northern neighbor.

Unbelievably, on the index of the overall crime rate, Alabama ranks fifteenth of the fifty states; New York ranks fortieth. Concerning the murder rate, Alabama is fifth in the nation. New York ranks twenty-third. Thus, one is much more apt to be murdered in Alabama than in the Empire State.

Concerning the crime of rape, Alabama ranks twentieth while New York is forty-eighth. Yes, that is right; New York is one of the least likely states for a girl or woman to be violated.

Also, a person from Alabama is slightly more apt to suffer from an aggravated assault than a New Yorker.

As for robbery, however, New York is much worse than Alabama. New York ranks third, while this Southern state comes in twenty-first of the fifty states.

Property crime, collectively, is a major crime index and contains burglary, larceny-theft, and motor vehicle theft. This state ranks fifteenth for property crime compared to New York's forty-fifth. That is, one is more likely to be burglarized, suffer from larceny and theft, and is slightly more likely to have his vehicle stolen if he lives in Alabama. Therefore, Alabama fares poorly next to the state with Albany as its capital regarding property crimes.

As for another aspect of safety, highway safety, I am afraid that Alabama is much worse than New York. Most people make fun of southerners when it comes to "snow driving," but this is more than just snow.

Yes, New York has more highway fatalities than Alabama but not a higher rate. We in Alabama are No. 15 out of fifty when it comes to the highway fatality rate. New York is forty-fifth; it is one of the safest driving places. When one realizes that over twice as many miles are driven in New York compared to Alabama, the difference is even larger than the rank indicates.

Moreover, alcohol plays a role in more of our highway deaths. In Alabama, alcohol is involved in four of ten highway fatalities, and only three in ten in New York.

Again, I offer this not as criticism but as food for critical thought.

Disturbing Events of Note in Iraq

Article #13
The News Courier, April 25, 2004

Several disturbing events have occurred recently, and many predict more ominous events. All have happened in Iraq. On Friday, April 9, thousands of Muslims were chanting against the United States. "Nothing new!" you may say. But this demonstration was different; it was new. The thousands consisted of Sunni and Shiite Muslims and were led by the Shiite Sheik al-Karbalie. That is like oil and water mixing. To write it politely, Sunnis and Shiites have not been best friends. Nothing unites two enemies better than when they both share a common enemy. The common enemy is us, the US. These changes may be the first faint sounds of a jihad. I pray to my God this is not so.

Thomas E. Ricks of *The Washington Post* reported the second alarming event. In the first week of April, an Iraqi battalion, the 620-man 2nd Battalion of the Iraqi Armed Forces, refused to go to Fallujah to support US marines battling for control of the city. The reason for their refusal? "We did not sign up to fight Iraqis," they insisted. If you follow events in Iraq, you know that one of the cornerstones of the occupation is to train and equip an Iraqi force to help establish order and tranquility.

Ricks continues his article and relates that in the last few weeks, 20-25 percent of the "Iraqi army, civil defense, police, and other security forces have quit, changed sides, or failed to perform their duties...." These events do not bode well for the American soldier.

The third disturbing event was the bombing by the occupational forces of a mosque. The reason for the bombing. It was used militarily by the opposing forces firing upon US soldiers. This situation poses a tremendous dilemma for our military commanders, who should protect our soldiers at all costs.

The zealous Muslims will not forget the mosque bombing. From zealous Muslims, terrorists tend to be born.

Finally, according to ABC News, Iraq's second-largest foreign army is not even an army. They are mercenaries (mercenary may not be the right term here). That is correct. Currently, these "hired soldiers" are second only to the US in the number of soldiers. There are more hired soldiers in Iraq than the entire army from Great Britain.

What government supervises these hired soldiers? None. They work strictly for private companies that do not answer to any government. They are hired, believe it or not, to protect US personnel and our soldiers in certain situations.

Some country, probably ours, will be held responsible for their deeds and misdeeds. I am not saying that the concept of privately hired soldiers is wrong. I am saying that the idea of privately hired soldiers who answer to no governmental authority is wrong.

A Growing Malignancy in the US Military

Article #14
The News Courier, May 23, 2004

A form of "cancer" is spreading in the United States military. It is not the fear of terrorists or the absence of bravery among our soldiers. It is non-military personnel operating within the military structure.

This malignancy, like a tumor, is infiltrating the body of the military and causing discipline to deteriorate. Its metastasis is through the command structure, transferring power to the wrong components.

"Malign" and "malignancy" have the same root word. To malign means to asperse or defame. Asperse implies a continued attack on a reputation, and defaming is an injury to one's good name. Civilian contractors are doing both to the US military. They are the malignancy.

There are approximately 20,000 mercenaries (hired guns) in Iraq. Some are even hired to protect the US military. Even though they supposedly are subject to military supervision, they are not covered by the Uniform Code of Military Justice, which means they play by their own rules.

USA Today quoted Thomas White, former Army Secretary, who said in a March 2 memo, "In the coming fiscal year, about one-third of the army's total obligation will be expended for contract support." Yes, one-third; the tumor is growing.

Deborah Avant, writing for *The Washington Post*, relates that during the first Gulf War (in which I served and served proudly), there was one civilian contractor in Iraq for every sixty active-duty personnel. At the start of the second war, there was approximately one contractor for every ten soldiers.

Currently, no one in the Pentagon, not even Rumsfeld, knows exactly how many contractors are in Iraq.

More alarming, no one knows the exact number of "contract prison interrogators." Thus, the Gannett News Service reported on May 17 that the CIA and Pentagon investigators are researching the possible involvement of these "contract prison interrogators" in the Abu Ghraib prison fiasco. The cancer is spreading.

A side thought: The beheading of Chris Berg was atrocious. My thoughts and prayers are with his family.

I have a simple question: Why was a young man in his twenties wandering the city streets in Iraq looking for employment? He was there trying to find work as a civilian contractor or sub-contractor. If the cancer were not so huge, he might still be alive.

A final thought— approximately three weeks ago, there was a huge turning point in Iraq. This resulted from myriad things, including the military and government "mindset" in Iraq.

The United States is no longer trying to win the war; it is now trying not to lose it. There is a huge difference between the approaches. One is offensive, and the other is defensive. Deputy Defense Secretary Paul Wolfowitz, appearing before the Senate Foreign Relations Committee on May 18, conceded: "...we and the Iraqis are stuck."

I firmly believe the Bush administration would leave Iraq tomorrow if they had a face-saving option. Forget democracy and freedom; they are no longer the main concerns. Pride is.

The Wall between Church and State Should Stand

Article #15
The News Courier, June 27, 2004

"Man prefers to believe what he prefers to be true," Frances Bacon once wrote.

Bacon's maxim is very correct regarding the beliefs of many Americans about the Christian faith of the Founding Fathers of our nation and the first few presidents. What many people believe about these men's faith is not true. Let me explain.

First, let us address the invocation issue at the Constitutional Convention of 1787 and the religious beliefs of three of the most important men there: George Washington, Benjamin Franklin, and James Madison. Second, I will examine the first few presidents' beliefs besides Washington and Madison. Then I will offer a final comment.

The Founding Fathers

The Constitutional Convention participants did not even invoke divine guidance for their deliberations. They never opened any session with prayer. Benjamin Franklin argued at a critical juncture in the sessions on the need for an opening prayer. The motion was strongly defeated. Franklin concluded that those who were present thought prayer was unnecessary, "except for three or four persons...."

James Madison, an important deputy at the Convention who eventually became the fourth president, wanted to ensure that no single religion became the state's religion and that church and state remained separate. In 1785 he wrote in his *Memorial and Remonstrance Against Religious Assessments,* "who does not see that the same authority which can establish Christianity, in exclusion of all other religions, may establish with the same ease any particular sect of Christians, in exclusion of all other sects." To Madison, church and state were like oil and water.

The First Few Presidents

According to *the Annals of America,* a twenty-volume historical collection, one of the "embarrassing problems for the early nineteenth century champions of the Christian faith was that none of the first six Presidents of the United States was an Orthodox Christian."

Unitarians believe in the unity of God (not the Trinity), the humanity of Jesus, and the ability of a person to overcome error by reason. Washington and Madison, the first and fourth presidents, have already been discussed. John Adams and John Quincy Adams were Unitarians, father and son, and the second and sixth presidents.

Thomas Jefferson, the third president and the architect of the Declaration of Independence, was, like Franklin, a strong and avid deist. Jefferson even produced a New Testament that deleted all miracles and reduced Jesus to only a great moral teacher and an extraordinary man. He contended that "Difference of opinion is advantageous in religion." In his famous *Notes on the State of Virginia,* he argued that neither a particular religion nor a particular sect of that one religion should have governmental or exclusionary power. Later, Jefferson wrote his famous letter to a Baptist church and argued strongly for the "wall" between church and state.

Freedom of Religion, Freedom from Religion

The Founding Fathers believed strongly that every American should have freedom of religion. At the same time, they thought the government should have and should be able to operate with freedom from religion. Worshipping one's God as one chooses was a very important individual right to these men.

We, as American citizens, should strive that NO sect "believing itself" possessed of all truth, and that every tenet differing from theirs …[is] error" should ever have "power… in their hands" and rule America. That is what the Founding Fathers envisioned and what we need to remember this July 4.

Some of you will prefer not to believe what I have written. You prefer to believe what you prefer to be true. But as Thomas Jefferson once said, "The truth will stand." The truth should stand, as should the wall between church and state.

Have You Seen Kerry or Bush Lately?

Article #16
The New Courier, August 1, 2004

As a citizen of Alabama, have you seen either presidential candidate lately? Don't worry; you won't. Why? Regarding the upcoming presidential election, we in Alabama are "nobodies." We are almost nonexistent to either party. The Republican Party thinks it has us in its back pocket (and they do), and the Democratic Party has written us off.

In an important card game, one should always play their cards close to their chest. Concerning the presidential election, Alabama has its cards stuck so far out that no one even "deals" with us or to us.

The presidential election is down to about ten states, and the chips of the other forty have already been cashed in, or "no cash in" in this instance. Neither party is sending major cash to Alabama. Why should they?

President Bush has visited over thirty times in one of the ten states. Yes, over 30 times, and it is not Texas. We in Alabama see him on TV. As for Kerry, I predict he may land his plane once in our state, spend maybe two hours at an airport, then fly far away.

Why is this? Because states have become more important than people in presidential elections. This is due, in my opinion, to the Electoral College system.

I have done the math for the 2004 election. Are you ready?

California and Texas, just two states, have more delegates than Alabama, Alaska, Arkansas, Delaware, Hawaii, Idaho, Maine, Mississippi, Montana, Nebraska, Nevada, New Hampshire, New Mexico, North Dakota, Rhode Island, South Dakota, Utah, Vermont, West Virginia, and Wyoming. Two states are worth more than twenty.

Some argue that the Electoral College system favors the rural states over the urban states. This is due to the apportionment of the delegates. Each state's Electoral delegates are equal to its number of US representatives plus its two US senators. Because of the "two senators" addition, sparsely populated states are thus over-represented.

On the other hand, eleven states controlled more than half of the Electoral College delegates for 2004. Win those eleven, and you are president. The other 39 states play "second fiddle."

I have read about the Electoral College system and how it dealt the cards in 1824, 1876, 1888, and 2000 presidential elections. I have also read the pros and cons of the Electoral College system.

Arguments for the system include that it requires a distribution of popular support to be elected president, enhances minority interests, and contributes to the political stability of our country by encouraging a two-party system.

Arguments against this method of electing presidents include the risk of electing a minority president, the possibility of so-called faithless electors, and reducing voter turnout.

After reading the arguments for both sides, the one thing that keeps gnawing at me is this: In the United States of America, each person's vote should count equally. It should not matter if I live in an urban or rural state. My vote should be as important as one from California or Wyoming. It is not.

From what I can gather, Pennsylvania may ultimately decide our next president. If Kerry wins the popular vote by millions but loses in Pennsylvania, according to the Electoral College card game, Kerry goes back to Boston. If so, the loser wins for the second time in eight years. This is not good for our country and will further divide an already divided nation.

So, my fellow Alabamians, during this presidential election, go ahead and throw in your cards, lean back in your chair, and turn on your TV. That is about as close as you will get to the candidates. If votes were truly equal, we might see them in person.

A Closer Look at Alabama's Family Values

Article #17

The New Courier, September 5, 2004

I waited to write this article until after the local elections. Some candidates who seek political office campaign by praising Alabama's family values and promising to support them if elected.

I write this now because I did not want it construed as favoring one candidate over another; it is written neither for nor against anyone. But let us look at our family values in this state. Maybe we should not run on them but from them. Please remember that I offer this not as criticism but as food for critical thought.

Family values should concern the entire family and the treatment of each individual from birth to death. Therefore, let us start with infancy. Who has more value than an infant? One in three children in Alabama is born out of wedlock, and one in ten is born with low birth weight, ranking Alabama third in that category. Moreover, Alabama is third in the nation in infant mortality rate. We rank very low in the care we give your youngest citizens, starting with nutrition when they are fetuses.

As the Alabama child ages, the care we give them ranks among the lowest in the nation.

We are sixth in the nation regarding the percentage of our children living in poverty and sixth in the nation for households headed by single mothers. Again, what values are we passing on to our young people?

As the Alabama child grows into their teen years, life doesn't get much better, especially for females. Our state ranks seventh in the nation for the teenage birth rate. Again, what happened to the values of which we are so proud?

As the Alabamian grows into adulthood, they face the reality that we are seventh in the nation in the divorce rate, ninth in the poverty rate, eleventh for receiving public aid, and sixth in accepting food stamps.

Furthermore, the value we place on personal debt payments cannot be praised. Believe it or not, Alabama ranks second for personal bankruptcy.

As we age in Alabama, our treatment as senior citizens is abominable. We rank second in the nation in the percentage of our senior citizens living in poverty and third in the nation for the age-adjusted death rate (Age-adjusted rates eliminate the distorting effects of population aging).

In my opinion, people running for political office in Alabama should campaign to improve our family values, not defend them.

They should address how to improve infant care, lift the Alabama child out of poverty and reduce teen pregnancy. We should search for new ways to improve the Alabama adult's life, help the family stay intact, and make us more accountable financially.

If I may paraphrase the novelist Ayn Rand, we may ignore reality. Still, we can never ignore the consequences of ignoring reality. Therefore, let us no longer ignore our real values and work together to improve them. (This information was taken from "State Rankings," thirteenth edition, edited by Kathleen and Scott Morgan, and published by Morgan Quitno Press.) Politicians—campaign on that.

People Should Have Candles to Illuminate Life

Article #18
The New Courier, October 17, 2004

When it comes to learning, a candle is much better than a flashlight. Flashlights brightly illuminate a small spot and lightly illuminate a surrounding area; all else is pitch dark.

Many people are like flashlights. They can shed light on a small area; all else is darkness. Flashlights and experts have a lot in common. They both can blind; one the eyes, the other the mind.

The candle, however, is different. It casts a warm, dim glow all around. It reveals just enough in all directions to make one want to look closer and learn more. It allows one to explore in any direction. It beckons with its soft glow and hypnotizes with its flicker. Wise people and good teachers are candles. Candles may be formally educated or not.

Let me give an example of a wise, uneducated candle that affected me tremendously. I was young, about twenty-five, and married to my first wife. We lived in Pulaski, and I worked at Martin Methodist College (now the University of Tennessee Southern).

My wife and I lived across the street from an elderly gentleman named Mr. Tidwell. He lived alone and was lonely. There is a difference, but he was both. He was misplaced, for he had been a farmer but now resided in a small apartment with an even smaller yard.

He still wore his overalls, cap, and work shoes. Sadly, he would walk in his yard, never stepping outside his boundary. To my knowledge, he did not have a family. He never spoke of one, and I never asked.

Occasionally I would wander across the street, and we would sit on his porch and talk. He had a second-grade education; I had a master's degree. I thought I was smart. I wasn't.

One day on his front porch, Mr. Tidwell and I were talking about the weather generally and the sun specifically. He then remarked, "Yeah, right now (June), the sun is setting over that tree, but come December, it will set over that," He pointed to a tree distant from the first one.

I sat for a moment, frozen in my thought. I, with my master's degree, finally responded, "Mr. Tidwell, the sun sets in the west." Mr. Tidwell, with his second-grade education, replied, "Yes, but it sets in different parts of the west."

That day Mr. Tidwell was a candle in my life. He beckoned me with his soft smile and hypnotized me with his flicker of wisdom. His knowledge of the sun and its connection to different "setting trees" at different times of the year revealed enough to make me explore.

Explore I did, and those "setting trees" became the solstice and equinox. Mr. Tidwell knew nothing of these words (neither did I at the time), but those were his trees. I had been raised on a farm but had never seen the forest for the trees.

Mr. Tidwell, may God rest his soul, lives on in my college classes. He speaks to my students through me. They learn about the solstice and equinoxes and why Christmas is three days after the winter solstice. I try to shed enough light to encourage them to look further. I, with my doctorate, try to emulate Mr. Tidwell with his second-grade education. I fall short. That lonely, misplaced farmer with a soft smile was a true candle.

Flashlights, experts, and master's and doctorate degrees shed a bright light on one small area. But candles spread soft lights in all areas, making us curious about God's creations. May you have candles in your life.

A Wound That May Not Heal

Article #19
The New Courier, December 5, 2004

Many requests for prayers for the American soldier occur every day, as there should be. But during the holiday season, I suggest we also keep their families in our thoughts. The Christmas season is especially difficult for the families of our service men and women. It is the separation from the families, sadly, that may later cause the separation of families. I write this because of first-hand knowledge. Let me explain.

During the Christmas season of 1990, my National Guard unit and I were activated for Desert Storm. The unit was a Mobile Army Surgical Hospital, and I was the executive officer. We left the United States on December 19. I witnessed many goodbyes before the flight. Wives were crying for their husbands who were leaving; husbands were crying for their wives who were leaving, and very sadly, many tears flowed from the small faces of children. Some children were old enough to know why, and some were not.

Unknown to most Americans, the military prepared for thousands of deaths and injuries. We landed in Frankfurt, Germany, and our hospital unit was immediately separated into approximately eighteen locations. We and other hospital units were scattered across Germany and Italy to provide medical care for military families and, very importantly, to receive the casualties from Kuwait. Administration offices were renovated in hospital buildings to receive casualties. At one location in Germany, thousands of caskets were waiting.

Fortunately, the casualties were few in Desert Storm. But there was another kind of casualty that occurred slowly. A type of wound that, in some cases, never healed.

One hears many proverbs in their lifetime. Two are relevant to this never healing wound. They are: "Out of sight, out of mind," and "Absence makes the heart grow fonder." Contradictory, aren't they? Most proverbs are. Which one is correct? Social psychology relates they both are; it just depends on the situation.

Many baby boomers and I are products of "Absence makes the heart grow fonder." My mother and father's love for each other grew during World War II. Their romance flourished during the war through letters while my father was stationed in the Pacific. This "letter romance" occurred countless times between countless couples. Why?

In World War II and the Korean War, very few women were on or near the battlefield. A man does not look on the other side of the fence if there is nothing on the other side, but he thinks of the one back home.

That is not true for Vietnam. Women were near the battlefield. That is not true for Desert Storm. Women were on the battlefield. And thus, in some cases, "Out of sight, out of mind."

Please do not misinterpret my words. I welcome equality and women to the battlefield. I have personally witnessed them with my fellow soldiers. It must occur sociologically, but psychologically it can cause problems.

Sadly, several fellow soldiers experienced separations and divorce months after our return stateside.

Recently, I read about a soldier fighting in Iraq who received a cell phone text message from his loved one. She said she no longer wanted to be with him and was leaving. He was devastated. "Dear John" or "Dear Johnnie" letters can be written from either side because either one can experience "out of sight, out of mind."

Thus, please keep military families in your thoughts this holiday season. They need them in more ways than one.

What Color Is God?

Article #20
The New Courier, January 16, 2005

The relationship between God and color is fascinating. I have been wondering about it since I was a little boy. I still wonder about it as a man, and now, it seems God is changing colors. Strange, isn't it?

As a little boy sitting in "theater-seat" pews during summer night revivals, I would stare at the picture of a white Jesus. I didn't know much then and still don't, but I thought people from the Middle East were more olive-skinned. *Maybe I am wrong.*

Reading American history books in elementary school convinced me that God must be white. He couldn't be red because "Manifest Destiny" meant the white European settler should replace the native red American. Push him from his soil and make him worship a white God; that was God's plan for America.

As I became older, I heard even more that God was white. I was told he could not be black because slavery was in the Bible. But I didn't know much as a teenager; I still don't. During my teen years, as black people struggled for equality, very few Protestant churches were in the trenches of the civil rights battle. In 2005, it seems that 11 a.m. on Sunday is probably the most segregated hour of the week.

From the latter nineteenth century until the 1940s, yellow didn't seem to fit God. In the early 1940s, most of the yellow people on our West Coast were herded together and sent to camps to ensure national security.

During the last few years, brown doesn't seem to fit God, either. Those coming from south of the border seem to want to replace the red, white, and blue of "Ole Glory" with red, white, and green—the Mexican flag.

Recently, I have been told that God has turned red. How? From what I gather, he now resides in the red states in America and stays out of the blue states. Those blue states are too immoral.

The red states know the Will of God better than the blue states. Blue states are too liberal, and God can't be a liberal. Red states are more God fearing, law abiding, and church going. I am unsure when God turned red; it seems it was between 2000 and 2004.

As a man in my fifties, my mind sometimes wanders back to those summer night revivals sitting in theater-seat pews staring at a white Jesus.

Maybe, just maybe, man is not made in God's image; maybe God is made in man's image. I didn't know much as a child, and I still don't.

Searching for Sophi in Ukraine

Article #21
The News Courier, March 2005

My wife and I are about to take a journey. We leave as two, and there will be three upon our return. The new addition will be "Sophi," a little girl.

Tracy and I are going to Ukraine to adopt Sophi. We have never seen her or even a photograph of her; we do not even know which little girl in Ukraine will become Sophi.

After many attempts with medical intervention and many thousands of dollars, we decided we can't have any more children.

Spencer is our soon-to-be-5-year-old bundle of joy. Tracy lost two early in the pregnancy.

I question why; she asks why I question. She accepts the losses as God's Will. She walks closer to God than I do.

Tracy believes God gave us Spencer so that we can adopt Sophi.

For months, Spencer has prayed to God to "drop a baby from heaven." When God chose not to, Spencer told me, "Well, Daddy, go to Walmart and get one!"

Why not try to adopt an American child? We looked into it in-depth, but the way the federal and state laws are written, we risked raising little Sophi and losing her later.

Thus, we are traveling to Ukraine.

Sadly, thousands of children in orphanages across Eastern Europe await adoption.

Abandoned by their parents, they are underdeveloped, malnourished, and under-loved. Tracy has faith that Sophi is there. She walks closer to God than I do.

Tracy has been emailing letters to Ukraine for months and letters and memos to American people who have returned from there. Some come back with children; some do not. She has crossed all the "t's" and dotted all the "i's" for documents, clearances, regulations, and everything possible.

For the past month, she has been buying little girls' clothes, sewing "little girl" patches on coveralls, purchasing dolls, and more. She has been getting Sophi's room ready with Spencer's help. She walks closer to God than I do.

She recently related the story of a four-year-old boy in Ukraine whose mother abandoned him because of bilateral hip dislocation. This condition can be surgically corrected. The little boy has an engaging personality and an infectious smile. A couple who just returned from Ukraine adopted a child with even more special needs and requested that some family consider this little boy. Tracy is. She would return with a plane full of children if I let her. She walks closer to God than I do.

So, Tracy and I leave soon; it will be our first separation from Spencer. Meemaw is coming to stay with him. We have been hugging him more lately. We have tried to explain it to him; he has tried to understand.

It will be a journey of encountering the unknown, dealing with judges and courts in a language we cannot speak or understand, and seeing many little faces pleading to be adopted. Please wish us God's speed and a safe return with Sophi.

I Found Faith and Hope in Ukraine

Article #22
The News Courier, April 10, 2005

In my last article, I related that my wife, Tracy, and I were going to Ukraine to try to adopt a little girl, who we would name Sophi. Not only did I find Hope in Ukraine, but I also found Faith. As I mentioned, Tracy walks much closer to God than I do. She had faith this was what God wanted. I hoped she was right.

To begin with, leaving Spencer, our five-year-old son, was difficult for us both. Meemaw and Peepaw, Tracy's mother and stepfather, came from Oklahoma to stay with him. Also, our friends Jody and Tammy Upchurch and Ray and Myra Rouse and their families helped keep Spencer busy and involved in his regular activities. Tracy and I are very grateful for them and all our friends.

Flying to Ukraine was long and tedious, with several stopovers. We were to be met by a facilitator at the Kyiv airport. After coming through Customs and Immigration, we walked into a small sea of people waiting on the passengers and speaking a foreign language. We walked past several people holding signs with last names. Nowhere did I see "Durm." I was becoming concerned. Finally, a young man in his midtwenties walked up to me. He asked in a non-Southern accent, "Are you Mark?" I said, "You better believe it!" The young man was Dima Subotenko. He became our companion for the next two weeks.

The following day we went to the National Adoption Center in Kyiv. We looked at books of photographs of unwanted children wanting to be adopted. We were shown two pictures of fraternal twins at one point. They were eighteen months old and had been abandoned by their mother at birth. Tracy wanted to see them.

They were in an orphanage in Kremenchuk, which is southeast of Kyiv. We hired a taxi and rode miles and miles through snow and ice, sometimes sliding and lost. Dima had never been to our destination. We arrived at 11:30 p.m., tired and stressed.

The next morning, we went to the orphanage. It was in a poor part of town in a multi-building complex painted a drab green. As we entered the door of the building that housed the twins, we could hear very small infants crying on our right. Different buildings housed different age groups of children. The only children Tracy and I saw inside the building were the eighteen-month-old group. The halls were narrow, dark, and foreboding.

It is hard to use ordinary words to write about extraordinary events. I cannot struggle to express how I felt in my heart. It was unfamiliar—an emotion Webster cannot define. There were rooms and buildings full of unwanted children waiting to be wanted.

As we sat in the orphanage director's office, Dima translated the circumstances surrounding the twins. As we listened, the door swung open, and two women arrived holding children. They were twins—Nadya and Vira. Vira clung closely to one attendant, and Nadya held the head and neck of the director so tightly that the director could hardly breathe. They were very scared.

Within three minutes, one of the twins, Vira, placed her small pale hand in Tracy's. We told the director we wanted to adopt them within two minutes.

According to the documentation, both had physical problems. Nadya had the most. The government of Ukraine does not allow foreigners to adopt healthy children. Now, neither Tracy nor I see the ailments.

For twelve days, Tracy and I, accompanied by Dima, went to many places, and signed many documents to finalize the adoption.

Vira and Nadya are Ukrainian names. In Ukrainian, Vira means "faith," and Nadya means "hope." Even though their mother gave them away, she had faith and hope that someone could give them a better life. Tracy, Spencer, and I would do our utmost. We named them Sophi Nadya and Sydni Vira.

Tracy, Spencer, and I now live in Doubleland—double diapers, double falls, double cries, double feedings, double trouble, and double joy.

Now, because my wife walks closely with God, she led me to Faith and Hope in Ukraine. Tracy, Spencer, the twins, and I thank everyone for their prayers, support, and encouragement.

America Needs More Purple People

Article #23
The New Courier, June 12, 2005

America needs more purple people. Purple people are in the middle and have been too quiet for too long. They are political moderates, conservative on some issues like red Republicans, and liberal on other issues like blue Democrats. Red and blue combined make purple. Red and blue beliefs make a person politically purple.

I believe most Americans are politically purple, but they are not passionate. They have neither the "my way nor the highway" mentality of the red, hot-collared radical right wing of the Republican Party nor the cold blue "I am smarter than you" obtuseness of the ultra-left wing of the Democratic Party.

The fabric of America is being torn in two by these two forces. We are no longer "a nation under God united," but instead a nation divided by divergent beliefs in God.

The purple people must rise up in the middle and reclaim their legacy. We should neither be intimated by the extremists nor softened by laziness. We should neither be satisfied to accept what happens nor complain about what does not occur. Fate is directed.

This great nation was founded on compromise; those who disagree with this have not read the minutes, written by James Madison, of the meetings of the Founding Fathers. If these men had not compromised, there would have never been a United States of America.

For example, the Constitutional Convention was on the verge of total collapse over the issue of representation in Congress. Should each state have equal representation? Should those states with more population have more representation? Roger Sherman offered what is known as the "Great Compromise." The United States Senate (equal representation) and the House of Representatives (more population, more representation) were born from this compromise.

Currently, the United States Senate and the Alabama Senate are at a standstill. Neither knows the color purple; both have lost the ability to compromise. Two weeks ago, in the US Senate, when a group of fourteen senators, led by Senator John McCain, found the color purple concerning judge appointments, they were immediately criticized by the extreme red and blue-wingers. What a shame. It was also a shame the purple majority did not rise up and praise them.

As for the Alabama Senate, it cannot even agree on a General Fund Budget. From what I can gather, the Democrats and Republicans are not even speaking to each other.

Aristotle spoke of the "Golden Mean." The dictionary defines it as "the median between extremes: moderation." Moderation is the path to follow. We have lost our way. America is deep in debt. It is also shallow in respect, both given and received.

Therefore, let the people in the middle take the best of the blue and red beliefs and forge them into purple. Let us color our way to respectability and acceptability. Let us stand tall and be proud to be purple. America needs us!

Admitting We Know Less About More

Article #24
The News Courier, August 21, 2005

The more I age, the less I seem to know. When I was young and knew everything, I heard wisdom comes only with age. Now I know that wisdom is knowing that one does not know everything or hardly anything. The older I become, the less I know about more.

The wise know there are no easy answers. The ignorant have many easy answers. The idealism of youth slowly fades into the realism of age. This brings me to my focus. I have become concerned about substituting "truth" for "faith."

Faith and truth are not synonymous, howbeit many religious leaders state otherwise. If something is proven to be true, then it is factual. If something is believed to be true but cannot be proven, it is a matter of faith.

The divergence of beliefs within Christianity, Islam, and other religions testifies that most are matters of faith, not truth. Why are there so many different Protestant denominations? Why the difference between Protestant churches and Catholicism?

Why the difference between Christianity and the Jewish faith?

They all claim to worship the same God. But how can that be? Is God the author of confusion? I think not. The problem arises because of faith differences, not truth differences. Truth does not vary.

I hear many ministers, priests, rabbis, and mullahs speak more of truth and less of faith.

Religions and denominations have every right to have a cornerstone of faith. None, however, have the corner on truth. I fear wider chasms are developing among religions and different denominations within those religions due to the substitution of truth for faith.

Many believe that truth will eventually emerge. Many of those people will submerge the truth if they do not agree with it. Often when individuals are questioned about their "truths," they respond, "Well, it has never been disproved!"

No one can prove a negative, nor should they. The positive proof of a statement falls upon the person who claims it.

During my life, I have met many people and taught thousands.

Those who think they know the most have usually been the most ignorant. Wisdom starts with awareness of not knowing; ignorance begins with no knowledge of not knowing.

When I give my students the orientation for the Critical Thinking class at the university, I say that if I do my job correctly, they will know less truth at the end of the semester. Many are puzzled by those words when the course begins; many understand and are pleased at the end.

Let us not confuse faith with truth. Again, faith can be different; truth does not vary.

As we grow older, let us grow wiser. Let us admit we know less about more. Maybe, just maybe, there will be more peace on Earth.

The History of Abortion

Part 1 of 2

Article #25
The News Courier, October 2, 2005

Since the nomination of John Roberts for the Supreme Court has brought the issue of abortion to the forefront, a historical overview of this procedure may be in order.

I write the following neither as justification nor condemnation of abortion. It is simply a look at its history. Therefore, there will be two articles. The first will focus on the era before the time of Christ, and the second one will focus on the period since the time of Christ.

Fiction: Abortion is a twentieth-century medical exercise indicating that people are becoming more immoral and uncaring.

Fact: Abortion (from the Latin aboriri meaning "to perish") has existed for thousands of years. One ancient Chinese work, supposedly written 4,600 years ago, prescribes mercury for inducing abortion. Another Chinese source, the 24-volume work entitled *Fu Ren Da Quan Liang Fang* (Encyclopedia of Effective Prescriptions for Women), written by Chen Zimin about 750 years ago, discusses prescriptions for contraception and abortion. In Book 13:7, the physician Chen writes: "Married women have difficulties at the time of childbirth. Some bear offspring unceasingly but desire to stop this. Therefore, prescriptions are written so they may be prepared for use."

Dr. Chen cites an earlier work entitled *Qian Jin Yao Fang*, which included a prescription called Qian Jin Qu Tai (Thousands of Gold Prescriptions for Abortion.) The concoction had barley leaves as the main ingredient and is approximately 1300 years old.

Ancient Greece also recognized abortion. Plato believed that the population of the Republic of Athens should be no more than 5,040 citizens. Aristotle stated, "If it should happen among married people, that a woman who already had the planned number of children to become pregnant then before she feels fetal life the child should be driven out of her." Plato and Aristotle thought abortion could limit the population and help maintain a stable economy.

Another well-known Greek, Hippocrates, the physician, gave a very clearly written description of septic abortion. Although one source relates that Hippocrates advocated violent exercise as the best method of abortion, he apparently strongly condemned the practice of interrupting a pregnancy without any medical reason. One part of the Hippocratic oath reads, "I will not give to a woman a pessary to cause abortion."

Ancient Hebrew culture is well-known to most people. Although the Bible never mentions abortion, a few verses are interesting concerning the nature of the fetus. The King James of Exodus 21: 22-23 reads as follows: "If men strive, and hurt a woman with child, so that her fruit depart from her, and yet no mischief follow: he shall be surely punished, according as the woman's husband will lay upon him; and he shall pay as the judges determine. And if any mischief follow, then thou shalt give life for life."

The Old Testament suggests that the fetus's life is less important than the mother's. If two men quarreling cause a pregnant mother to miscarry, the guilty one should pay a fine to the woman's husband. If the expectant mother, however, is killed, then the guilty one must die also. It could be argued that the ancient Hebrews did not give equal status to the unborn child.

In the Old Testament, this unequal status is more explicit in Numbers 5: 24-28. A woman accused of adultery is required to drink "the water of bitterness" (an abortifacient possibility?), "And he shall cause the woman to drink the bitter water that causeth the curse: and the water that causeth the curse shall enter into her, and become bitter. And when he hath made her to drink the water, then it shall come to pass, that, if she be defiled, and have done trespass against her husband, that the water that causeth the curse shall enter into her, and become bitter, and her belly shall swell, and her thigh shall rot: and the woman shall be a curse among her people. And if the woman be not defiled, but be clean; then she shall be free, and shall conceive seed."

If the woman aborts, she is adulterous and made a curse and an oath among her people. But Numbers 5 offers no indication of concern for the unborn. It seems mother and unborn child did not have equal status among the Hebrews.

In the next article, I will discuss the history of abortion since the time of Christ.

Sources: The Westminster Dictionary of Christian Ethics, James F. Childress and John Macquarrie, Editors; International Handbook on Abortion, Paul Sachdev, Editor; The Holy Bible (King James Version); The Catholic encyclopedia, Charles G. Herbermann, et al., Editors; Collier's Encyclopedia; Free Inquiry, "Anti-abortion and Religion" by Betty McCollister; Abortion in America: The Origins and Evolution of National Policy, James Mohr.

Abortions History Since the Time of Christ
Part 2 of 2

Article #26
The New Courier, October 9, 2005

Last week we looked at the history of abortion before the time of Christ. In this article, we will look at the history of abortion since the time of Christ.

The New Testament does not specifically mention abortion, but it does discuss the rejection of evil drugs and potions (Gal. 5:30; cf. Rev. 9:21; 18:23; 21:8; 22:5). Some of these verses seem to mention abortifacients, but that is not certain. Two treatises written at the same time as the New Testament but considered noncanonical strongly condemn abortion and infanticide. These works were entitled Didache, or Teaching of the Twelve Apostles, and the Epistle of Pseudo-Barnabas.

Condemnation of abortion was prevalent in the early church. Clement of Alexandria (c.150-c.215) grouped abortion with sexual immorality and opposed using abortifacient drugs. Tertullian of Carthage (c.150 – after 220) wrote against using abortion to hide a pregnancy. Tertullian called abortion to save a woman's life a "necessary cruelty." He emphasized his belief that the fetus was alive before birth.

Even though condemnation in the early Christian church was widespread, Tertullian, Jerome (c.347-c.420), and Augustine (died around 607) believed there was a difference between the formed and unformed fetus and a difference between the ensouled and unensouled fetus. These early church fathers believed that the body is not formed into a "man" (or woman) until sometime after conception. They accepted the possibility that God did not infuse the soul until the body was formed. Thus, abortion before ensoulment would not be a homicide, per se, but would still be sinful. According to one source, Augustine believed the fetus was ensouled at forty-six days. However, he abhorred the abortions of both formed and unformed fetuses (Dictionary of Christian Ethics). Another source relates that this ensoulment process (also called the "quickening" doctrine) was proposed by Aristotle and accepted by Augustine and Thomas Aquinas

(1225-1274) and that the process was forty days for male fetuses and eighty days for females (Beth McCollister "Anti-abortion and Religion").

Thomas Aquinas wrote in his Summa Theologiae III that a person who caused an abortion by striking a pregnant woman was guilty of homicide only if the fetus was formed, that is, forty days if male and eighty days (one source reads ninety days) if female. Aquinas placed the lives of the mother and the formed fetus on an equal status. He rejected killing the mother to baptize the fetus, even though the formed fetus's external life may have been at stake.

This difference between the formed and unformed fetus was influential in discussions in the Catholic Church until the eighteenth century. In the eighteenth century, the Catholic Church shifted to believing that the fetus should be protected from conception. As for the Protestant Reformation, both Luther (1483-1546) and Calvin (1509-1564) held that both soul and body existed immediately at conception. Melanchthon (1497-1560) believed that God gave the soul only after the fetus was formed (40–80 days).

Chronologically we now come to the history of abortion in America. An excellent source for this is a scholarly work by James Mohr entitled Abortion in America: The Origins and Evolution of National Policy. Mohr writes that abortion was openly accepted in America until about 1850 (abortion did not even become a statutory crime in England until 1803). The practice was questioned in America because of concern over the number of abortions by medical quacks. The challenge came from the American Medical Association, not America's religious institutions. The Medical Association scolded the churches in America for not being active enough on this issue. Thus the Supreme Court decisions of the 1970s did not represent the weakening of moral standards but rather a return to what had been.

Sources: The West Minister Dictionary of Christian Ethics, James F. Childress and John Macquarrie, Editors; International Handbook on Abortion, Paul Sachdev, Editor; The Holy Bible (King James Version); The Catholic encyclopedia, Charles G. Habermann, et al., Editors; Collier's Encyclopedia; Free Inquiry, "Anti-abortion and Religion" by Betty McCollister; Abortion in America: The Origins and Evolution of National Policy, James Mohr.

Evolution: Is It the Handiwork of God?
Part 1 of 3

Article #27
The New Courier, February 5, 2006

We should acknowledge evolution because life evolved. Plain and simple. Contrary to what you may hear, the process, the "what" of evolution, is a proven fact. It is all around us, day in and day out.

Part 1 of 3

It is the "how" of evolution where theory comes into play. There is the basis of Charles Darwin's "natural selection" theory, Stephen jay Gould's "punctuated equilibrium" theory, and others.

I predict the resistance from the church to evolution will slowly fade, just as the belief that the earth was flat and the sun revolved around the earth slowly faded.

The world is round, and the earth revolves around the sun. Why?

Well, I believe it is the handiwork of God. So, in my opinion, evolution is the handiwork of God.

I have often wondered what God thought during the Middle Ages, looking down on the round earth revolving around the sun and, simultaneously, the highest, most ordained members of religion and royalty proclaiming it was flat and the center of the universe.

Whew! These exalted "called" members accused anyone of blasphemy if they differed.

What did God think? What does God think? What does God think now about the creation scientists?

The Institute for Creation Science in San Diego, CA, has been the leading proponent and promoter of the Creation Science concept. The institute has spearheaded the bills introduced and passed in various state legislatures in America.

The institute does not allow academic freedom for its members. It makes them pledge that they believe in the factual and historical interpretation of the Bible.

Such as every living species on the earth was created suddenly during the six days described in Genesis.

My argument is based on the term "creation science." I have no problem with the term "creation religion;" one has an inalienable right to have religious beliefs of his or her choosing.

If one argues that God created the world supernaturally, that is his/her right, thus "creation religion." But if one argues "creation science," one postulates the natural creation of the universe. If one believes in creation science, one must take leave of his logical faculties. Logic is one of the highest orders of thinking and is the result of the evolution of our brains. It is a God-created talent (through evolution). What parent would give his child a toy and then tell him not to use it?

I will write this argument for evolution on two fronts. In my next article, I will offer four premises against creation science. In the third installment, I will include two premises for evolution.

My premises against creation science occur not with Adam or Eve but with Noah. Through the ark builder, one can disprove creation science. Seeing the dilemma caused by the flood epic, some creation scientists believe there was evolution after the flood but not before. As I see it, that is akin to thinking a woman can be half pregnant.

The four premises against creation science will be (1) the size of the ark and its cargo, (2) the number of people to load the ark, (3) the number of days to load the ark, and (4) the amount of rain.

Concerning my two premises for evolution, in the first, I give historical examples of evolution, including color blindness, sickle cell anemia, and goosebumps.

The second Premise will discuss present-day examples; the cotton aphid and the A H3N2 influenza strain, to name just two.

Until next week and Noah...

Evolution: Is It the Handiwork of God?

Part 2 of 3

Article #28
The News Courier, February 12, 2006

Last week I argued that God might want us to believe in evolution. This week I offer my four premises against the concept of "Creation Science." Again, I do not argue against "Creation Religion" because religion is based on supernatural beliefs. Science, however, studies the natural order of things.

Second of Three Parts

Proponents of creation science argue that the evolution of species never occurred and that Genesis is to be taken literally, not figuratively. If so, God created all species that have ever lived and that were alive during the first six days of creation. Some semi-creation scientists propose that a "day" of the first six may not adhere to twenty-four hours but may be much longer. Even if that belief is accepted, creation science posits that all living species alive today were created by the end of six "days."

To wit, if creation science is correct, then all species that have ever breathed life had to be on Noah's Ark! Thus, I will offer my four premises against creation science by relating that the flood epic could not have happened naturally, scientifically that is (remember, last week I wrote that some creation scientists realize that the ark epic unravels their theory and therefore believe that evolution occurred after the ark, but again, this is akin to believing a woman can be half pregnant).

Premise No. 1: The ark was too small to hold all species of life. In Genesis 6:15, the Living Bible reads, "make it 450 feet long, seventy-five feet wide, and forty-five feet high." Thus, the volume was about 56,250 cubic yards. The cargo (or 'passenger list') was astronomical. Based on the number of known species in the major groups of all organisms, the list had to include: 30,800 protozoa, 26,900 algae, 69,000 fungi, 4,800 prokaryotes (bacteria and similar forms), 1,000 viruses, 281,000 animals (times two because of male and female), 751,000 insects (times two because of male and female), and 248,400 higher plants (plants cannot naturally live under 17,000 feet of water (explained in Premise No. 4).

Also, notice I listed only the 751,000 species of known insects. According to sampling tests, when done in forests, there are 10 to 30 times this number of species not known. Thus, there may be 20 million species of insects.

Think for a minute—tuberculosis, HIV (AIDS), the syphilis bacterium, the gonorrhea bacterium, the herpes virus, the bird flu virus, and all other present-day maladies had to be on the ark if there is no evolution.

How could Noah have stored these diseases? In tubes, Petri dishes, or what? Remember, creation science says he did it naturally, not in a supernatural way.

The above numbers, which are very conservative (no one knows the actual number of all species on Earth), do not even consider how Noah and his family fed all those beings. Remember, there must be a natural explanation.

Premise No. 2: Noah and his family were too few. There were only eight people to do all this loading. There was Noah, his wife, their three sons (Shem, Ham, and Japheth), and their wives (see Genesis 6). By my conservative calculations, each would be responsible for "naturally loading" over 270,000 life forms and over 30,000 plants. Need I write more? Before I leave Premise #2, let me address another matter about the number of animals loaded on the ark. Those who read the Bible closely (these I admire) know there are two contradictory accounts in Genesis about the number of animals. In this article, I use the more accepted account. Besides, if one prefers the "seven pairs of clean animals and seven pairs of unclean animals," that person believes in evolution. There are more than fourteen species of animals on Earth.

Premise No. 3: Noah and his family were not given enough time to load the ark. Genesis 7: 4-10 says the loading of all these species was to occur in seven days. Eight people in seven days?

I am not trying to be flippant but serious when I ask: How could penguins from the Antarctic region get to the Middle East within seven days? Or the slow-footed armadillo from Texas, or slow-footed turtles from anywhere? How could they swim the ocean?

Remember, creation "scientists" say there is a natural explanation, not a supernatural one. Need I write more?

Premise No. 4: It could not have rained naturally over 17,000 feet in 960 hours. Genesis 7 says it rained for forty days and forty nights (40 x 24 hours) which equals 960 hours, and "all the high mountains under the entire heavens were covered. The waters rose and covered the mountains to a depth of more than twenty feet" Mount Ararat, in the part of the world where Noah supposedly lived (present-day northeastern Turkey), is 17,011 feet high. So if I add twenty feet to the 17,011 and divide by 960 hours, the creation scientists want me to believe that it rained almost 18 feet per hour!! Need I write more?

Yes, I do. Close Bible readers will note Genesis 7:11 where, besides the rain, "...all the springs of the great deep burst forth...." But this statement is based again on an erroneous ancient Hebrew belief of a small flat land Earth floating on an enormous flat ocean.

So, to conclude this installment, if one is to believe in the creation science natural world, one must not only take leave of their logical faculties but also throw away common sense.

Next week will be the argument for evolution through the examples of cotton aphids, sickle cell anemia, goose bumps, color blindness, and Type A H3N2 influenza. Until then...

Durms Final Thoughts on Evolution's Evolution
Part 3 of 3

Article #29
The New Courier, February 19, 2006

Last week I offered four premises against creation science. Today I give two premises for the belief in evolution.

Last in Series

Premise No. 1: People today reveal historically advantageous traits that may now be disadvantageous. For example, color blindness in men (there are seventeen times more color-blind men than women) was an advantage when people had to hunt for food. Why? If a man is color-blind, he is a better hunter. The camouflage that animals try to use to hide from the hunter is of very little use if the hunter is color-blind! Thus, evolution naturally selected (natural selection) this as a positive trait.

In World War II, the US military wanted bombardiers (they sat in the belly of the plane and dropped bombs) to be color-blind. This bombardier could still see the outlines of the enemy's camouflaged jeeps, tents, and other equipment. Today, however, being color-blind is disadvantageous. We get our meat from the local grocery but drive through red and green lights to get there! Some men can only tell traffic signals apart by their brightness. I have a distant cousin who is this way.

Sickle cell is another trait that is beneficial in natural selection but harmful if the selection is removed.

In the remote past in Central Africa, people were dying from malaria to the extent that the dreaded disease was decimating the population. Nature needed a mutation that would be resistant to malaria; the sickle cell was its selection (natural selection). The sickle cell prevented the population's extinction by allowing the species to live long enough to reproduce. Now, it is a dreaded genetic disease. African Americans who have sickle cell anemia are descendants from Central Africa. Malaria is not prevalent in the United States, so the sickle trait is a liability.

And now a question: Why are you blinded by suddenly turning on a light after you have been asleep? Or conversely, why can you not see anything in a dark room if you have been in the bright sunlight but can slowly see more things the longer you stay in the darkened room? Remember stumbling in the old days in a theater after the movie had started? Well, it takes time for the pupil of the eye to completely open up or close to pinhole size. Why? Because the sun rises and sets slowly. Your pupils know nothing, evolutionarily speaking, about instantaneous electric light. Electricity has not been around long enough for the eyes to adapt that quickly!

What about goosebumps? They were and still are advantageous. You get them on two occasions, when you are scared and cold. Why? Well, goosebumps make your hair stand on end, and when that happens, you appear larger to your enemy, and you can withstand cold winds better. Goosebumps were an evolutionary advantage when we had more body hair and didn't wear clothes. They are still advantageous because we shiver when they occur, increasing body heat.

Premise No. 2: There are many examples of ongoing evolution occurring in the present time. A very relevant example of this is the cotton aphid (Aphis gossypii). The cotton aphid's pesticide resistance is well-known among farmers and extension agents. This strong resistance results from natural selection, a key premise of evolution. During the summer, a pesticide that kills this aphid on June 1 may not even make a dent in the population by July 1. Why? Because there are several generations of this aphid in one summer, possibly as many as one per week. During the summer months, the females have live young without the males being present.

Another good example of present-day evolution is the A H3N2 influenza strain. Let me quote an article by Daniel Yee from The Associated Press that was in newspapers nationwide in mid-January. "The government, for the first time, is urging doctors not to prescribe two antiviral drugs commonly used to fight influenza after discovering that the predominant strain of the virus has built up high levels of resistance to them at an alarming speed." "[T]he predominant strain this season—the Type A H3N2 influenza strain—was resistant to older drugs." "[I]t may have been the result of a mutation in the virus or overuse of the drugs abroad...." One flu expert, Dr. William Schaffner of Vanderbilt University, said the development was 'disconcerting' as flu now has joined the ranks of other diseases, such as tuberculosis and HIV, that recently have acquired the ability to resist front-line medications."

"Mutations," "resistance," what is occurring here? Simple—evolution. Flu viruses are evolving around the medications; more "bugs" resist front-line medications."

In summing up, let me restate my conclusions. For me to believe in creation science, I must agree that:

Eight people in seven days loaded over one million species of organisms and hundreds of thousands of plants (plants cannot live for days under 17,000 feet of water) on a 56,250 cubic yard boat.

That it rained almost eighteen feet per hour for 960 hours.

That sickle cell anemia is a condition God put on people from Central Africa from day one; which son of Noah did they descend from that carried this sickle cell?

That all races of humankind are descended from eight people. Have you ever wondered which one of Noah's sons was black-skinned? Which one was white? Which one was yellow? Which one was red-skinned?

I don't believe that the A H3N2 influenza strain was on board the ark but did not appear until the twenty-first century. Real scientists have a term for creation science; it is called evolution. I believe God wants us to believe in it; it is His handiwork.

The Majority of Americans Favor Abortion

Article #30
The News Courier, April 23, 2006

Let us take a closer, cooler look at a highly heated topic—abortion. Abortion is one of those topics that the extreme purists on both ends of the political spectrum (the ultra-conservatives and the ultra-liberals) continually keep in the media, giving the impression that American society is highly divided. It is not.

Contrary to what you might think, most Americans favor abortion under certain circumstances. Poll after poll and study after study have shown that the overwhelming majority of Americans consider congenital defects, rape, and maternal health threats sufficient grounds for abortion. Conversely, personal convenience and gender selection are not sufficient.

Most Americans are in the middle, but television talk shows and newspaper headlines dislike moderation. Media love controversy, not civility. One of the biggest points of contention between the ultra-conservatives and ultra-liberals centers around the question, "When does life begin?" The arch-conservatives believe life begins at conception; the left liberals believe it is later in development. All people would agree life occurs at birth. In my opinion, the ultra-conservatives are more concerned about life before birth than after birth. If I could be reassured that all unwanted babies would be adopted into a loving home, I would be against abortion. But I live in the real world. There are buildings full of them in America and other nations. I do not understand why, if one is so adamantly pro-life, they don't adopt children who are already alive and unwanted.

Contrary to what many people think, overturning *Roe v. Wade* is overturned will not outlaw abortion. It will allow all fifty states to pass legislation favoring or opposing it. If it is overturned, there could be fifty different sets of rules.

Last month there was a scientific sample taken by *USA Today*/CNN/ Gallup representing all of America. The poll asked, "Would you favor or oppose a law in your state that would ban all abortions except those necessary to save the life of the woman?" 60 percent of all respondents opposed such a ban on abortions, and 36 percent favored it.

Surprisingly, in the South, 62 percent opposed such a ban against abortions, higher than the national average. Thus, as I have stated, most Americans favor abortion under certain circumstances.

Morris P. Fiorina makes a compelling point in *Culture War? The Myth of a Polarized America,* when he claims, "not everyone who believes that abortion is wrong... supports making it illegal." Fiorina further adds that from 2002-2003, five different polling organizations conducted eight surveys. Each poll asked a version of the "most important problems facing the country." None—I repeat, none—of the polls received enough abortion responses to report it as one of those "important problems."

Many of you who read this will not agree with the research findings. Many prefer to believe what they prefer to be true. Many prefer gut data over good data.

It is hoped, however, that concerning abortion, the great majority in the middle will be more vocal, energized, and resistant to purists on each end.

Then I Have a Very Good Mother

Article #31
The New Courier, May 14, 2006

On this day, Mother's Day, I would like to honor mine.

To my knowledge, my mother has never stood to receive any awards or acclamations, nor has she ever sat on any board of directors. But she sat beside me as a child and stood with me as a young man. For that, I love and respect her very much.

No one has ever opened an office door with my mother's name, for she has never been an executive. But if a good mother takes her family to church whenever the doors open, I have a very good mother.

My mother has never worn fancy clothes or brand names. But if a good mother can cut and sew cloth and make garments for her children that are the envy of their peers, then I have a very good mother.

My mother has never read any of the great books, not Shakespeare, not Voltaire, or Rousseau. But if a good mother reads the Good Book daily, I have a very good mother. Her Bible is worn, dog-eared, noted, underlined, and starred.

My mother has never dined at The Four Seasons or any fancy restaurant. But if a good mother knows how the four seasons affect the garden— when to prepare, plant, hoe, and harvest- then I have a very good mother. My mother has even fed fresh tomatoes to her family at Christmas time!

My mother does not have a college degree or a high school diploma. My mother has never written an article or even an essay. But if a good mother writes letters to her son when he is away from home, then I have a very good mother. My mother has never stayed out late at night or been where she shouldn't be. But she would never sleep until both teenage sons were home at night, safe and secure, praying they had not gone to places they shouldn't have gone.

My mother breastfed me when I was an infant, corn-fed me when I was a boy, and fed and fed and fed me when I was a teenager. She once remarked I could eat more than any human being she had ever known. If good mothers cook and cover the table with food, I have a very good mother.

I know that my mother's days and hours are numbered. Her body aches from arthritis, and she is plagued with diabetes. A stroke has dimmed her mind, but her spirit and soul are still beacons of light for her family and all who come in contact with her. She toils on and never complains.

I do not see eye to eye with my mother on all things, but I respect her vision and foresight in everything. Odell Hatchett Durm is my mother—she is a very good mother, and I love her very much!

The Biggest, Strongest Man in the World

Article #32
The New Courier, June 18, 2006

If there is any good in me, it is due to my mother and father. The bad in me is due to me. This past Mother's Day, I wrote of my mother. Since today is Father's Day, please allow me to write about him. As a small child, I thought he was the biggest and strongest man in the world.

Throughout my life, he has been there, both physically and emotionally. When I was a child, he kept me safe and secure. As a teenager, he allowed me to make mistakes. As an adult, he allowed me to choose my own life.

He has been a man of few words but many thoughts throughout his life. He has no college degree. I have several, but he is still my teacher.

I love and respect him for all the times he said something when he should have. I also appreciate all the times he did not say anything when he could have. Those were times when nothing was spoken, but everything was understood. He could say more with his eyes than most can with their tongues.

My father, a deacon, does not wear his religion on the outside as so many do. Instead, he lives it on the inside as so few do.

"Pap" is a member of the World War II generation. He worked two jobs, one as an office machine mechanic and the other as a farmer. I often observed him entering the door after finishing his public job only to change into his farm clothes. He never sat down between jobs. He, like most men of that era, is not outwardly affectionate. He does not speak of his love for his family, again a man of few words, but he expresses it through his actions.

My father was very proud of me when I played football, although he never said it. At fourteen, I told him I wanted to play; he said that was fine, but I had to find my way to practice. We lived sixteen miles from the high school. I rode my bicycle. After a week of this, he said, "You want to play, don't you, son?" He was testing me.

He taught me not to waste time and that it was better to be an hour early than a minute late.

He taught me not to waste money; a penny earned is better than a dollar not earned.

Darwin Lee Durm will be 84 in October. His health is declining, but he is still the biggest and strongest man in the world.

An Alarm Clock, a Bank Robbery, and Lightning

Article #33
The News Courier, July 30, 2006

What do an alarm clock, a bank robbery, and lightning have in common? Simply odds. Odds that are related to gambling.

I remember witnessing a sad event several years ago in Georgia. Tracy and I were on vacation. I stopped for an overnight stay. I went jogging and finished my run at a local convenience store. I entered to buy a soda. Standing in front of me at the counter was a young lady in her late teens or early twenties, buying "one more" lottery ticket for five dollars. As she was buying it, she told the clerk she had hocked her only alarm clock at the local pawn for five dollars, and her husband would be upset when he got home.

Recently, I stopped to get gas at a convenience store in Tennessee. As I entered to pay, there were two middle-aged ladies who, it seems, were spending their last few dollars on lottery tickets. I should not be judgmental, but by their dress and demeanor, it seemed the money could have been spent better elsewhere.

It seems to me, and now I am being judgmental, that we have a problem in our country that has become cancerous. This cancer affects all ages. People are becoming addicted to gambling, and those who suffer from this affliction can afford it the least.

Sadly, internet sites can feed their addiction twenty-four hours a day. The sites are not even regulated.

Many young people, too young, can wager. According to a recent study by the University of Pennsylvania's Annenberg Public Policy Center, online betting among college students has increased five times over the past four years. Every week, almost 600,000 people under the age twenty-two wager online. What is this teaching our young people?

Does anyone care?

Greg Hogan learned the hard way. Greg, at nineteen and a Lehigh University student, robbed a bank in Pennsylvania. Why? He was attempting to pay off a $5,000 debt from playing online poker.

Many of my students at Athens State admit to gambling when I discuss probability theory in my statistics class. I ask if they would bet on being struck by lightning in Alabama. All say, "No." I then relate that they have a better chance of being struck by lightning in this state than winning the lottery in Tennessee or Georgia.

Some who read this will think I am against an Alabama lottery. If I am, it's because I am more against anyone hocking alarm clocks to purchase "one more chance" instead of buying needed clothes and necessities.

Why would anyone bet on something when they have a 99.9999 percent chance of losing? Granted, chances of winning in Biloxi or Tunica are better than winning the lottery, but what kind of example is being shown to our children and grandchildren? Maybe the young are learning to wager regardless of the odds. Oddly, they may realize that alarm clocks can be used for other reasons. There are other reasons for robbing banks and betting money on occurrences that have less probability than being struck by lightning. "Against all odds" may become their new motto.

Saying 'Just Charge It' Is Dangerous for the US

Article #34
The New Courier, October 26, 2006

Let the buyer beware! We are not aware, and yet we buy and buy.

In the old days, you could not get a soda, go to a movie, or buy anything unless you could pay cash. Not so anymore. No need to beware if you do not have the cash to buy in the first place.

Now you can purchase a cup of coffee, a candy bar, go to the movie, or anything else, and you do not even have to have one shiny red cent. How? All you need is a credit card.

Credit card companies are now letting people make purchases of less than $25.00 without requiring a signature. Individuals are now "charging" burgers, deli sandwiches, milkshakes, and even packs of gum.

Credit card companies want you to move through the checkout line quicker, use a card to pay for everyday items, and increase the debt you owe them. In the past six years, this less than $25 charge has increased tenfold for the Visa credit card alone. Yes, you read it right—TENFOLD.

Credit card debt has quadrupled in the past sixteen years—from $200 billion to $800 billion. What are we, who are older, teaching those who are younger? If one leads by example, I am afraid we are leading them to fall. Fall into debt that is.

Some of my students, by age twenty, have already accumulated a staggering credit card debt. Some college students even pay a 20 percent interest rate on their debt. What does a 26 percent interest rate mean? If no payments are made, it means that what is owed will double in two years and nine months.

Our national debt has doubled in the past five years. More alarming, in the past twenty-six years, it has increased eightfold! Not only are we individually careless with what we spend, but collectively it is heartbreaking and a disgrace.

Consider, for example, that in 1990 you owed $10,000. You work at your job and try to do your best. But this year, 2006, you wake up one morning and realize you owe $80,000. (Honestly, I don't think most Americans have awakened to that fact.) You wonder what has happened. Simple, "you"—

Americans—have been spending more than you are saving. Americans are probably the greatest spenders and the worst savers worldwide.

China, you know, the country of bicycle riders, buys our country's bonds. You get it; the US pays interest to China to keep our economy afloat. Odd, isn't it? But let us not worry or fret about this. We gas-consuming Americans borrow from the bicycle-riding Chinese. Just "charge it."

Simply put, my dear reader, the US cannot continue on the economic path we have chosen for the past quarter of a century. We must become aware. We must wake up.

Children's Bodies Growing Adult at Early Ages

Article #35
The News Courier, February 25, 2007

News Bulletin
State of Alabama
Year: AD 2127
A six-year-old female has just given birth to a baby.

You read it right. It is predicted that a six-year-old child will give birth to another child in approximately 120 years. And not only in Alabama but across the nation and in other countries with high socioeconomic status.

"Impossible!" "Will never happen!" are the reactions I usually get from my students when I teach this in Adolescent Psychology and Physiological Psychology at Athens State. But when I explain what is happening physically and biologically to our young people, my students' reactions are collectively one of alarm.

Let me explain, but first, let me relate little-known facts; in 2002, a ten-year-old girl gave birth in Alabama and probably conceived during her ninth year.

That year, the youngest father in Alabama was twelve, possibly siring the child at eleven. In 2004, the youngest mother in this state was eleven; in 2005, age twelve.

This phenomenon is called the "secular trend" in our species.

Our young girls in America and other parts of the world are starting menstruation (menarche) earlier at the rate of four months for every ten years of calendar time. Thus, do the math; a ten-year-old girl now giving birth, a nine-year-old in 2037, an eight-year-old in 2067, a seven-year-old in 2097, as the news bulletin exclaimed, a six-year-old in AD 2127

I am not being flippant when I say young ladies in high school today look much more mature than when I was going to high school. Let's look at it from another perspective. A young lady at age twelve today has the same physically developed body as her great-grandmother did at age fifteen.

This is also true for boys. To my knowledge, when I played football in high school, our team had the second-largest player in the state. He weighed

235 pounds! He played tackle; today, there are halfbacks this size. A young man played high school football weighing over 400 pounds approximately five years ago! Those players did not exist in my high school days.

It is believed that spermarche (the presence of viable sperm) occurs earlier in young men at the same rate, but it is harder to document than menarche.

Among the many myths most people believe is that in the 1700s, 1800s, and early 1900s, people married and had babies earlier.

Not so! If you do not believe me, check the data and the "average" age of marriage and parenthood in those times.

America has been collecting data on the secular trend since approximately 1900. In the US, in 1900, the average age of menarche for a young lady was fourteen. Norway has kept the best records of this phenomenon. In approximately 1845, the average age was over seventeen. By 1970, in Norway, it had dropped to thirteen.

Dr. Michael Freemark, Chief of Pediatric Endocrinology at Duke University Medical Center, claims, "Young girls [in the five to 10-year-old range] with breasts or pubic hair are encountered daily here in the clinic."

Why is this secular trend happening? As some people think, it is not all of the growth hormones pumped into cattle and chickens or all the food additives. Check the beginning dates in the above paragraph; no hormones or additives existed in those early days.

Why do we, as a society, have this problem? I think it results from a high-protein and high-fat diet. We eat more, get bigger quicker, and sexually mature faster. The brain's hypothalamus (the body's thermostat) monitors the body's weight. Each individual's genes give a person a range of height and weight. The environment controls where you place on the genetic range.

For example, let's say John Doe is genetically given a low range of five feet, 2 inches tall (this height will occur if there is very, very little food to eat) and a high range of six feet, 2 inches (will occur in a high-protein, high-fat diet).

As we evolved, the hypothalamus set an "average weight" point of 105 pounds in the human female to start menarche (notice again, this is an average; one-half begins lighter than 105 pounds, one-half heavier). But, because we eat such a high-fat, high-protein diet, our species is reaching this 105-pound average much quicker. Thus, the hypothalamus, tied to its evolution, thinks the young lady is several years older than she is, and as a result, menarche occurs.

A blatant example of this effect became apparent after the introduction of McDonald's hamburgers in Japan. The average Japanese teenager has gained ten pounds!

Another poignant example involves a football game. On October 23, 1903, Auburn played Alabama at Montgomery's Highland Park. The average weight of Alabama's players was 148 pounds. For Auburn, the average weight was 161 pounds.

To conclude, our young children's social environment creates the problem (diet). They are psychologically children but biologically adults. We have a dilemma. What do we do? What happens if we do nothing?

News Bulletin
State of Alabama
Year: AD 2127
A six-year-old female has just given birth to a baby.

Where Have the Fathers Gone?

Article #36
The News Courier, March 11, 2007

Is there ever a time when it would be better for a little boy if his father were dead rather than alive? Yes, according to one study done several years ago. In this particular study, it was revealed the little boy suffers fewer emotional problems if he could say, *"If my father were alive, he would take me to the ballgames and go hunting and fishing with me,"* than not be taken to ballgames or activities even though the father is alive. It is better for children to have been loved in the past than not in the present.

This is just one study, and one doesn't make a law; it makes one wonder, "Where have the fathers gone?"

Where are the fathers in our society? An increasing number of babies are born out of wedlock, and the number has reached an all-time high. In 2005, in the US, nearly four out of ten babies were born without the father being married to the mother. To be "illegitimate" is no longer illegitimate in our society.

Even though the teenage birth rate has dropped to its lowest level in recorded history, nearly 80 percent of all teen births now are to unwed mothers. In 1970, it was only 30 percent of all teen births. The number of births to unwed mothers in their twenties has risen to unforeseen numbers. In the year 2000 in the US, 50 percent of all births to women ages twenty to twenty-four were outside marriage. As the new mother gets older, illegitimacy drops substantially. Since unwed mothers are mostly young, the institution of marriage will become less sacred as those mothers age. Suppose this trend continues at its present rate. In approximately twenty years, one-half of all newborns in the US will have a father who is not married to their mother. Maybe the mother does not want the father to marry her! More and more women want a baby, but not its father.

Furthermore, the increase in illegitimate births is seen in all racial groups but has risen most sharply among Hispanics.

By profession, I am a psychologist and believe little boys and girls need fathers. I base this on many, many studies. A physically absent father causes many absences in his child's life. Fatherhood does not end at conception. It begins at conception. Siring a child is fun and easy; raising a child is fun and hard.

Some fatherless children try to hide the hurt, but emotional pain is not a game of hide-and-seek. Every hour a father spends with his child becomes timeless when the child grows into adulthood.

Concerning time, the future of this country depends heavily on fathers who are present for their children. In 2007, with almost 40 percent of children born out of wedlock, what does the future hold? I again ask, "Where have the fathers gone?"

Gun Control: Is It the Answer?

Article #37
The New Courier, April 22, 2007

After the tragedy at Virginia Tech, our nation is left asking, "Why?" and "What can we do to stop this kind of violence?"

Supposedly, and sadly, the "why" was due to a self-pitying and violent individual who blamed the university and its students for his problems. These violent tendencies were evident long before the tragedy, and Virginia Tech's professors, police, and counseling office had tried to help the young man.

The answer to the second question, "What can we do to stop this kind of violence?" is a much harder question. What can we do?

After the tragedy, I started researching the issue of gun control. Is this the answer? And just like my conclusion for many other issues, I know that I don't know. I researched both sides, pro and con, and, at age 56, I am growing so tired of each extreme side "spinning the truth," not only on this issue but on most social issues.

For example, the anti-gun research states the following: "Europe, which has much stricter gun control laws than the United States, also has a much lower rate of gun-related deaths. The rate of gun-related deaths in the United States is eight times higher than that of other high-income countries." (www.veganpeace.com)

The pro-gun advocates counter with the following: "the facts show that there is simply no correlation between gun control laws and murder or suicide rates across a wide spectrum of nations and cultures... A comparison of crime rates within Europe reveals no correlation between access to guns and crime." (www.cato.org)

Contradictions, thus, where is the truth? Probably it is in the middle. But as in most cases, the middle of an issue is always too quiet. The middle of society is also always too quiet and not passionate enough to argue, and thus we all lose.

Another example of this spinning the truth concerns the restrictive licensing of handguns- weapons that can be concealed. The pro-gun proffers the following information: "The thirty-one states that have... laws allowing private citizens to carry concealed weapons have, on average, a 24 percent lower violent crime rate, a 19 percent lower murder rate, and a 39 percent lower robbery rate than states that forbid concealed weapons." (www.cato.org)

The anti-gun proponents, however, argue the following about concealed weapons: "studies strongly suggest that restrictive licensing could have a positive effect on lowering the number of gun-related problems... the District of Columbia... study concluded that restrictive licensing of handguns was associated with an immediate decline in homicides and suicides by guns in the District of Columbia." (www.veganpeace.com)

Again contradictions. Each side uses statistics to contradict the other side. As stated before, the truth is probably somewhere in the middle. But again, the silence of the middle is deafening. The middle does not have "fire in its belly." The middle is afraid it might offend someone by speaking out on social issues.

And while we remain silent, thirty-three people just lost their lives at Virginia Tech.

In 2006, five Amish school children were shot to death; in 2005, seven were killed at Red Lake High School in Minnesota; in 2002, three were shot to death at the Appalachian School of Law; in 1999, thirteen were killed at Columbine High School; and the list goes on and on including Pearl, Mississippi, and Richland High School in Giles County, Tennessee.

In conclusion, we have difficulty answering the second question: "What can we do to stop this kind of violence?" I offer a third related question: "Why does this kind of violence, children and young people shooting their own in school, tend to occur only in America?"

I know that I do not know.

Maybe We Need to Lose and Fail More

Article #38
The News Courier, May 27, 2007

Maybe what is partially wrong with society is that we do not lose enough. Maybe if we lost more, we would end up winning more. Abraham Lincoln and Harry Truman did.

One often hears the slogan, *"Winners never quit, and quitters never win."* This is not entirely true. Bill Gates quit college and is now the richest man in the world. When it comes to money, I believe Ol' Bill has won.

Many people in the world are miserable because they will not quit. Just think of all the people who stay in miserable, mind-numbing, melancholy-causing jobs. They just cannot bring themselves to quit and look for something else that may be more enriching. They have the *"quitters never win"* philosophy. Thank goodness Abraham Lincoln was not like that. Lincoln failed and quit as a store clerk and storeowner in New Salem, Illinois. And, oh yes, Harry Truman wasn't like that either. Truman failed and quit as an owner of a men's clothing store in Kansas City. Both were quitters and are ranked in the top five of all US Presidents. By quitting, they won.

Maybe we should allow people to fail more. A test of character and integrity is not how one handles himself when he wins but when he fails. To handle winning with dignity is easy; to handle losing with dignity is difficult. Character is forged through adversity, not advertisement.

In my opinion, America's educational system is failing our children by not allowing them to fail. When a student is passed, regardless of the quality of work, what are we teaching the child? Attendance and achievement are not synonymous. Unbelievably, for many students who enroll in my senior collegiate-level classes, it is their first class in which they may fail. In elementary school, middle school, high school, and community college, they were passed even though they could not do the work. Many will argue that if you fail a student, you will damage his or her self-esteem. Does not this process teach our children to blame someone else or society for their failures when they become adults? Could this have been one factor in the tragedy of West Virginia? Did not the assailant blame society for the wrongs in his life?

This past spring semester, I had a student taking my statistics class for the third time. He remarked, "Dr. Durm, I finally understand it." He passed and graduated. Would I not have done him and society a greater disservice by passing him in the beginning when he did not understand? By failing, he won.

How should we teach our children to pray? Should we ask God to prevent us from falling or for help getting up when we have fallen? Falling is a part of life. Even as a toddler, it teaches us better balance, so we're less likely to fall the next time. I argue that losing teaches more respect for winning. One doesn't appreciate the mountaintop until he or she has walked in the valley.

We each have our talents and areas in which we may have no talent. Maybe if society would allow us to fail, we could find our true talent and thus win.

Better to Be Ready Than Proverbial

Article #39
The New Courier, July 15, 2007

Let me write something very proverbial. Do not let proverbs lead your life. Sounds contradictory, doesn't it? But that's the point; proverbs are contradictory. Let me explain.

When it comes to affairs of the heart, some people believe "Out of sight, out of mind." Others, however, give credence to the concept, "Absence makes the heart grow fonder." Totally contradictory.

As for affairs of opportunity in life, many will espouse, "Look before you leap." At the same time, others propose, "He who hesitates is lost."

Or about the proverb, "Better safe than sorry," compared to "Nothing ventured, nothing gained." Confusing, isn't it?

How about those timeless proverbs concerning time? "You can't teach an old dog new tricks," but wait a minute, what about "It's never too late to learn." Seems chronologically confusing, doesn't it?

What about achievement, that is, getting things done? Do we accept "Two heads are better than one" or believe "Too many cooks spoil the broth?"

How about the judgment of character? Is it more correct that "You can't tell a book by its cover" or "Clothes make the man?"

So, what should be used if one should not use proverbs as anchors in life's journey?

I believe one should consider what I call the Abraham Lincoln philosophy. I read, many years ago, a statement penned by Lincoln when he was young: "I will prepare myself, and if the opportunity ever comes, I will be ready."

He did. It did. He was.

Preparation for life involves analysis. It is very wrong, in my opinion, to raise a child with the belief that "You can do anything you set your mind to." Better to invite them to ask, "What are my strengths and weaknesses?"

A child should be taught, "You can do anything you set your mind to as long as it is within your abilities." Some of my students disagree with me when I teach this.

Imagine telling a child with an IQ of 100 that he can be a brain surgeon if he tries hard enough. The parent is setting up the child for the two F's – frustration and failure. It ain't going to work, folks.

Therefore, finding your strengths is very important.

"Prepare myself," as Lincoln wrote. But what about: "If the opportunity ever comes?" This is the more difficult one; no one can control all the variables in life. No one has ever chosen parents, place of birth, or where one lives in the first years of life. Someone else chooses these variables.

But there are also variables we can control. Who we marry, where we go to college, where we work, whether we use drugs, whether we commit crimes, and whether we save money or spend it needlessly. The list could go on and on.

Thus, control those variables as you can, and more opportunities will come your way. Or, if I may use a country euphemism, "Get the ducks you can control in a straight row; some ducks you can never control."

Finally, if you prepare yourself and the opportunity does come, you will be ready. Better to be ready than proverbial.

Man Deserves Some Credit, Not Just God

Article #40
The New Courier, August 26, 2007

Many of you have heard the phrase, "God helps those that help themselves." The phrase is not in the Bible to the best of my knowledge, but I agree. I would also like to share some thoughts about this phrase. Namely, Man deserves some credit too.

I think "Those that help themselves help God" and "Those that help others help God even more." Man deserves some credit too.

Recently in Meridianville, Alabama, a five-year-old boy almost died from eating lettuce at a Huntsville restaurant. The lettuce contained *E. coli*. The young lad suffered kidney failure and had three weeks of dialysis at a local hospital.

When a local television station interviewed the boy's mother, she related the prayers offered on his behalf saved him. She never mentioned nor gave thanks to any of the doctors, nurses, or specialists at the hospital. Giving thanks to God is great, but giving thanks to all the hospital personnel is also good. These medical personnel spent countless hours, days, weeks, months, and years studying and preparing to help others. They sat alone in rooms with books while others watched television and had a good time. Thank God for book sense. I desire never to be operated on nor attended to by medical personnel without a good book sense education. Do you?

Some may argue that God should get all the credit because doctors, nurses, and specialists get their abilities from God. But my point is that they did something with the abilities they were given because of hard work on their part. Many people never fulfill their promise because of laziness. As Thomas Edison once said, "Most people miss opportunity because it is dressed in overalls and looks like work."

I believe God helps those who help themselves and loves those who help others. What matters most about prayer—its "upward mobility" or its "inward mobility?" Should we always turn our "problems over to God," or should we also tackle them ourselves?

Whose action is more justified in God's eyes? That of a man who only prays that the hungry be fed but never lifts a finger nor a dime to feed them, or that of a man who helps feed the hungry but never prays for God's help? I believe the best approach is to lift a finger and pray. But of the two, which is more justified in God's eyes?

Humankind is beset with many problems, and many are because people sit on their behinds. People deserve some credit, not just God. In my opinion, God is big enough to share the credit for good things. He probably would like to share it with more people. So, I thank God for those people who have denied themselves to help others. I thank God for medicine, science, and medical personnel and scientists. Religion should embrace science and medicine, for they make our lives easier.

Discussing an Unrecognized Injustice

Article #41
The News Courier, September 30, 2007

Something appalling happened in a remote corner of the world. It was not reported by any of the major media. Its occurrence, however, comes from a very reliable source.

All the men of an ethnic group were killed, every single one of them. The victors captured all the women and children and took all the possessions of the vanquished group. The victors even burned the towns of the defeated.

When the victorious army returned with its spoils and captives, their tribal leader was very angry with them. What happened next should be a travesty to those in every civilized nation in the world.

The leader said to kill all the boys and all the women who had ever had sex with a man. The only remaining group, the young virgins, were kept and divided among the victorious army.

Why was the tribal leader so angry? Why were all the men, all the young, innocent boys, and experienced women killed? According to this leader, they worshipped the wrong god and tried to instill this god into the belief of his people. The victorious leader said his deity instructed him to do this as vengeance on these people.

Before the above ghastly event, adding insult to injury, the same leader invaded a different region and removed the people who lived there. He seized all of their property, claiming his deity had given the land to him and his followers. Can one imagine a man and his family tending their ground and raising their herds to have them taken away by an invading tribal leader claiming it was his God-given right? Where was the United Nations when all of this was happening? Why weren't the human rights organizations protesting? Where was man's appeal to decency?

Well, there was no UN and no human rights groups.

Who was this leader that ordered this killing and invasion, all done in the name of his deity?

It was Moses. The invading and killing army was the Israelites, and the deity was the God of the Old Testament. I personally find it difficult to worship the God of the Old Testament. Read Numbers 31 in the Bible, and you may understand why.

I am not quoting out of context.

We easily and appropriately condemn Al-Qaeda, Hamas, the Taliban, and other groups for killing innocent people.

We easily condemn them because they worship a different god. But why is it so difficult to condemn the same acts when people who worshipped our God committed them?

Is it possible that this is the kind of hypocrisy Jesus referenced when he said in Luke 6:41-42 (also Matthew 7:3-5): "Why do you look at the speck of sawdust in your brother's eye and pay no attention to the plank in your own eye?... You hypocrite, first take the plank out of your eye, and then you will see clearly to remove the speck from your brother's eye."

Before he admonishes his audience, Jesus stated (Luke 7:39): "Can a blind man lead a blind man? Will they both not fall into a pit?"

Is the world falling into a pit at the beginning of this twenty-first century?

'It's Only Money?' Federal Government Must Prioritize How It Spends

Article #42
The New Courier, October 28, 2007

Old men make wars, young men fight wars, and young children suffer the consequences.

President Bush vetoed the plan to expand the State Children's Health Insurance Plan. When he spoke against the expansion, he claimed the extension would have benefited families earning as much as $83,999 a year.

Bush's statement was incorrect for forty-nine states in the union; it was correct only for New York, where the cost of living is extremely high.

Would you think denying a family in Huntsville making $36,820 this expansion of children's health coverage is wrong? Probably not, since the average cost of private health insurance for a family of four is $12,000 per year. But $36,820 in Huntsville equals $83,000 in Manhattan when you factor in the cost of living.

If you do not believe me, check any cost of living index. Money is cheaper in some places of America and more expensive in others. Bush knew this but never spoke of it.

Moreover, to Bush, money is more valuable in some places than others. If SCHIP had become law, it would have cost $35 billion over a period of five years, or $7 billion a year.

This $7 billion would have provided medical care for countless children in America. But approximately two weeks after Bush vetoed this medical coverage of children, he requested from Congress an additional $46 billion for the wars in Iraq and Afghanistan, and he wanted the $46 billion before Christmas!

Thus, as I have stated, money is more valuable in some places than others—$36 billion over five years compared to $46 billion in two months.

Suppose Congress approves this extra $46 billion. In that case, the total cost, so far, of the wars in Iraq and Afghanistan would be $650 billion, or almost two-thirds of a trillion dollars.

It is hard to grasp the number "one trillion;" it is a one followed by twelve zeros. If each dollar spent on the present wars was one second, two-thirds of a trillion seconds is equal to 21,104 years! Again, it is almost incomprehensible. A trillion is such a large number that only politicians use it; mathematicians do not.

Can the country continue these expenditures if we cannot afford medical coverage for our children? I do not write this because President Bush is a Republican; I would write it if he were a Democrat, an Independent, or whatever.

Unbeknownst to most Americans, the US borrows money from China to stay afloat. We who ride in SUVs are borrowing money from people who ride bicycles. Now that is a hellish picture.

But do not worry, it is only money. Or is it? Are we sacrificing the future and health of our country? Which is cheaper, money or the future of our children?

The Millionaire Next Door
Part 1 of 2

Article #43
The News Courier, November 22, 2007

Typical millionaires are not whom you think they are. They are more apt to wear a Timex watch than a Rolex and live well below their means. Eighty percent of America's millionaires are first-generation rich. More than half have never received as much as $1 in inheritance. How do I know this? Read "The Millionaire Next Door: The Surprising Secrets of America's Wealthy" by Thomas J. Stanley and William D. Danko; it is an eye-opener. The book is based on a thorough analysis of millionaires across America. What occupation has more millionaires than any other? Not lawyers, not medical doctors, not engineers, but auctioneers. They became millionaires and remained so by budgeting and controlling expenditures. As the book relates, those who are wealthy work to stay financially fit. They efficiently allocate time, money, and energy in ways conducive to building wealth and keeping it.

Thus the foundation for building wealth can be summed up in three words—FRUGAL, FRUGAL, and FRUGAL. Most people will never become wealthy in one generation if they are married to people who are wasteful. Financially independent people are happier than those in their same income and age group who are not financially secure. Thus, money may not buy happiness, but it sure reduces its cost.

Again, the typical millionaire is self-made. Fewer than one in four ever receive "an act of kindness" of $10,000 or more from their parents, grandparents, or other relatives. Nearly half never received any college tuition from their parents or other relatives, and 91 percent never received, as a gift, as much as $1 of the ownership of a family business. They paved their own road to wealth.

Children, Grandchildren, and Money

All parents should read this book. Children and money do not always go together. The more dollars adult children receive, the fewer they accumulate, while those given fewer dollars accumulate more. Giving money to adult children causes them to spend more than they save and invest. Also, adult children who receive gifts from their parents often do not distinguish between their wealth and the wealth of their gift-giving parents. Furthermore, adult children who receive gifts are significantly more dependent on credit than non-receivers.

You Are Not What You Drive

How about those people who act rich but are not? The book uses the slogan "Big Hat No Cattle" to refer to this group. There is an inverse relationship between the time spent purchasing luxury items such as cars and clothes and the time spent planning one's financial future. If you spend more time thinking about the big hat than the cattle, you may have the hat, but that is all you will have.

This article examined the traits of millionaires who may live next door, those who have paved their road to wealth.

Next week I want to discuss the "interest brick" that may help you pave your road, especially if you are a young adult, and how you can become a millionaire in your own house.

The Millionaire in Your House

Part 2 of 2

Article #44
The News Courier, November 29, 2007

Last week I wrote about how "The Millionaire Next Door," those present-day people who have paved their road to wealth by using a few simple bricks. This week I would like to examine the "interest brick" that has two components, the interest that works for you and the interest that works against you. Knowledge of this brick is very important if you are a young adult, and it may make you a millionaire in your own house.

In my Critical Thinking class at the university, I lecture for one week on money matters and how, with self-discipline, they can become millionaires. I also discuss this particular "interest brick." Let us begin by examining how interest works for you.

Would you, the reader hire me for all thirty-one days for the month of December and pay me only one penny on the first day and double the amount each day? For instance, you would owe me two pennies on the second day, four cents on the third day, and so forth. Would you?

If you did, on the thirty-first day, you would owe me a total of $21,474,836.48! Yes, you read it right, over $21 million. If you do not believe me, just do the math. This is one of the strongest pavement bricks on the road to wealth—it is known simply as "compound interest." Compound interest and the "Rule of 72" are twins.

This rule of seventy-two is simple. Whatever interest your money makes (whether it be in savings, stocks, or whatever), you divide the interest rate into seventy-two, and that is how long it will take your money to roughly double. For example, if you are receiving 6 percent on your money, it will take twelve years to double in value (72 divided by six equals twelve). Eight percent will double in nine years, and if it secures 12 percent, it will double in six years. Therefore, if a young person at age twenty-five invests only $5,000 at 6 percent, it would amount to $160,000 at age eighty-five. If this young person takes that same $5,000 and invests it at 10 percent, it will be worth $2,000,000 at age eighty-five. You may argue, "I will not live to eighty-five." Well, if you live to age seventy-eight, you are still worth $1,000,000. (The stock market has averaged 10.4 percent annually for the past eighty years.)

Now, to that other side of the "interest brick," the one where interest works against you. This concept of "amortization" is one of those things that is almost hidden. Many banks and loan companies wish you would never be knowledgeable of this. To amortize, according to the dictionary, is to "provide for the gradual extinguishments of a mortgage by contributing to a sinking fund at the time of each periodic interest payment." An amortization schedule is a table that lists the *monthly payment, principal* and *interest* amounts, and the unpaid *loan balance* for each month for the life of the loan. If you prepay or add the principal for the next month or several months, you save the interest shown for those payments *over the life of the loan; however, you still must make the full payment for the next payment.*

For instance, if you prepay the principal on two payments on a 15-year mortgage note (180 months of payments), you have reduced the payments to 178 at the end of the loan. Some mortgage companies will "penalize" you a small amount if you do this. Thus, you now see why the banks and loan companies do not want you to do this. My advice is never to secure a loan that has a prepayment penalty.

To conclude, the road to wealth is paved with a few simple bricks if you are willing and disciplined to travel it.

American Revolution

Article #45
The News Courier, December 20, 2007

I recently received a flier from a car dealership in the mail that blazoned, "Good Credit! Bad Credit! No Credit! No Problem! All credit applications will be accepted."

The buyer could pay $29 and drive home any car on the lot. Yes, all credit applications would be accepted, but the small print reads, "Subject to credit approval." It was misleading at best and unethical at worst. The flier declared the opportunity an "American Revolution." That it is, but in my opinion, not one that is desirable.

One day, I witnessed the epitome of this "revolution" while listening to a car commercial on the radio. The person was screaming for everyone in radio land with bad credit or no credit to "come on down," and they would be welcomed. At the end of this thirty-second, screaming commercial, the gentleman said softly, "and those with good credit, we want you too."

The flier and radio commercial were totally about the quantity of credit and nothing about the quality of the cars—an American revolution. This kind of revolution also occurred on the home mortgage front.

I have a personal anecdote here, too. I received in the mail one day a credit reference for one of my rental tenants. The tenants were applying for a mortgage to buy a house, and I was proud of them. After checking my payment records, I wrote an honest assessment: "Tenants do pay monthly but have been late at times."

Approximately one week later, I received a phone call from the loan officer. She said, "Mr. Durm, because of your statement, they will not be able to qualify for the loan. Could you change it?" I was stunned. I had told the truth. Should I lie? The lady faxed me another loan reference.

I sat in my office and reviewed the payment records. I faced a dilemma. I did not want to prevent them from owning a home. So, I responded as a politician. I didn't lie, but I didn't tell the full truth. They were able to buy the house.

The scenario is an example of sub-prime mortgages. I've wondered if this meant credit references in America for those mortgages were asked to respond at a sub-prime level of truth—an American revolution.

This December, the Treasury Department reported on mortgage default rates nationwide. The US average is 19.69 percent.

Almost one in five house mortgages in America is failing.

Yes, America is having a revolution. Because of credit cards, we spend money we don't have. We buy houses we can't afford, and people with the least money purchase cars at the highest interest rates. If you think nobody cares, try missing a couple of payments.

To Live Is Costly...Capital Punishment is Even More Costly

Article #46
The News Courier, February 3, 2008

As I have written in my columns, "common sense" often leads one astray. Executing a criminal convicted of a capital offense seems like it would save taxpayers money.

The cost of feeding and housing a criminal for life compared to sudden death seems extravagant. But, according to many different studies, it is not.

This column is not written for or against capital punishment.

I do not have difficulty executing a person if that person has factually taken innocent lives. The words "factually taken" are important here. Being sentenced to death is not morally right if the person did not kill anyone.

To date, with the advent of DNA testing, 120 people on death row have been exonerated. That is scary and should be sobering to prosecuting attorneys.

But let us get back to the taxpayers' money. The death penalty is not cheap.

This past fall, one of my students, Valerie Hayes, conducted an excellent study in my Critical Thinking class. Her research revealed the following:

- A 2005 study in California found that each of the state's executions cost the taxpayers $250 million. Unbelievably, the California death penalty system has cost the people of that state $114 million per year more than what would have been the cost of life imprisonment.
- In one of the most comprehensive studies ever done, Duke University found that for the state of North Carolina, the death penalty costs $2.16 million more per execution than the cost of life imprisonment for the same murderer.
- In Florida, the total annual cost of the death penalty is $51 million more than prison without parole for first-degree penalty murderers. In Texas, a single death penalty case costs $2.3 million. That amount is three times the cost of imprisoning the murderer in a single cell for forty years at the highest security level.

- In Indiana, according to an Indiana Criminal Law Study Commission, the complete cost of the death penalty exceeds, by about 38 percent, the total costs of life without parole, assuming that one in five death sentences are overturned and shortened to life imprisonment.

But enough of the studies, a simple question should be, "Why is capital punishment so expensive?" Because of the cost of court appeals used by the convicted.

For instance, an analysis of the legal costs to defend indigents in the state of New Jersey revealed the following: $509,765 in salaries, $126,959 in court reporters, $761,376 for mitigation specialists, $21,758 for litigation support, and a whopping $891,094 for attorneys hired when the public defender uses outside representation. This amounts to $2,310,952 per criminal.

A perfect example of such expenditures is the case of Brian Nichols. On March 11, 2005, during his trial in Atlanta, he shot a trial judge, a court reporter, a deputy, and a federal agent. There were eyewitnesses. He later surrendered live on television.

Because he faces the death penalty if convicted, his trial has been delayed five times. His case alone has exhausted the funds available to defend indigents: $1.5 million of taxpayers' money.

To live is costly, but to die is even more costly for the convicted. It is costly for the taxpayers. Doesn't make common sense, does it?

Things That Are True and Things That Are Not

Article #47
The News Courier, February 17, 2008

Searching for truth can be very elusive. Much of what people believe is not true, and many things people do not believe are true. There is another category, however. Many things are true and not true. In such instances, a basic understanding of statistics can be helpful.

Many of you believe that suicide rates among teenagers are higher than other age groups because suicide annually ranks as the second or third leading cause of death among teenagers. This belief is espoused by teachers, ministers, and the news media. But the belief is true and not true. Suicide is the second or third leading cause of death among teens yearly. It is not true that they commit suicide more often than other age groups. The opposite is true; teenagers commit suicide less often than any other age group. If you do not believe me look at the data. How can this be?

Suicide is a leading cause of death among teens because they are healthy. Thus, they do not die of cancer, heart attacks, strokes, and so forth nearly as often as older people. Their health pushes suicide higher on the list of causes of death.

Another example of this tricky category would be accident-prone driving. Many believe that we become reckless car drivers as we get closer to home. Why? The statistic often quoted for this belief is that 90 percent of all auto accidents occur within ten miles of home. So, presumably, recklessness increases the closer we get. This is true and not true. Approximately 90 percent of all vehicle accidents do occur within this ten-mile radius. However, it is not true that we become more reckless. Actually, the opposite is true again. We become safer drivers as we get closer to home. How can this be? Most do not realize that approximately 95 percent of all driving occurs within ten miles of home. If the location had nothing to do with accident proneness, then ninety-five, not ninety, percent of all accidents should occur within the same ten-mile radius. Thus, the accident rate decreases as we get closer to home.

Have you ever wondered how television channels 19, 31, and 48 can claim to be number one in the Tennessee valley? Well, it is true and not true. Here, one must read the fine print. Each station is number one at some time of the day. For example, channel 19 may be number one at 6 a.m., channel 31 at 12 noon, and channel 48 at 6 p.m. I am not sure which one is number one at which time because the claim is made in print too tiny to read. But that is why their claims are both true and not true. Number one at some time of the day and not so at other times.

In conclusion, claims can be both true and not true, and it is tricky to figure out why that is possible. A basic understanding of statistics is helpful. If one does not understand statistics, one will be abused by statistics. On a broader scale, such abuse is called politics.

Understanding the Stopped Watch Syndrome

Article #48
The News Courier, March 16, 2008

Last month, my father fell and broke his hip. As his body ages, his mind slowly grows younger and more childlike. It is difficult to watch. A once proud and strong man with a razor-sharp, mathematical mind now needs someone to balance his checkbook.

When Dad went for three weeks to the rehabilitation center wing of a nursing home in Lynchburg, TN, I noticed a pattern among the patients there. I call it SWS—the Stopped Watch Syndrome. Like a stopped watch, time has stopped for many of these people. If you think about it, change helps us perceive time. If one's life is the same every day, time stands still. If you awaken in the night and it is still dark, it is the same night; if you awaken and dawn greets you, it is a new day. Some, like watches, have white faces, some black. Some have faces once adorned with silver or gold or sprinkled with diamonds. Now, the glow has diminished, just like watches. Some have faces whose owners once preferred simplicity; others only wanted to serve. Their watchbands were made of military cloth.

These people once had hands that kept people on time; made sure children were where they had to be. Hands that once said it was time to work or relax now never work and only relax. Hands that made sure people ate on time are still waiting to be fed.

Just like stopped watches, they have faces that once were watched constantly but are now rarely, if ever, looked at. Other people pass without so much as a glance.

They, like stopped watches, feel useless. Few people listen to them because they are only right twice a day. They, like stopped watches, once were taken everywhere but now are kept in dark and hidden places. Many don't know not if it is day or night. Is it 6 a.m. or 6 p.m.? Does it matter? Rarely do their hands and faces feel the warm sun and fresh air.

Like some stopped watches, their battery and heart, if you wish, works. Other parts may not. The heart ticks, but the hands don't move as they should.

My father and mother will be moving to Athens soon. We hope Daddy's watch has more time and ticks and the parts still work. We hope he will still feel the fresh air and sunshine on his face and hands and not be placed in a darkened room. We hope my children will bring a smile to his face and a warm, loving pat from his hands. We hope he will enjoy some quality of life before the watch stops. We hope for these things. It is difficult to watch.

It Was His Time to Go; It's Easier to Believe in Fate

Article #49
The News Courier, May 4, 2008

Have you ever asked your son or daughter to study for an exam to make a better grade, and they responded, "Ah, Mom (Dad), why study? I am going to make what I am going to make."

"If she is meant to be mine, she will come back." Who hasn't heard this from someone who has experienced a romantic breakup?

You may have heard my favorite, "It was his time to go."

For example, people might say when a friend has died in an automobile accident, "Well, if he had been sitting at home, he would have died; it was his time to go."

I have heard all of the above. In each situation, the individual has an external-locus-of-control belief. They believe God, fate, or whatever controls our destinies.

People vary on whether they believe their life is inner-directed (internal locus of control) or outer-directed (external locus of control). The student who thinks the amount studied for a test is directly related to the grade on the test is inner-directed; he believes that what controls his life is located inside him. If one commits to "getting back" a romantic partner, one also has an internal locus of control. He credits his determination or motivation for outcomes.

This locus of control concept exists on a continuum. The degree to which one imagines control as inner or outer varies. Most fall along the continuum rather than at one end of the other. A completely external individual would believe in predestination, the notion that one is predestined to go to hell or heaven from conception. A total internal believer would believe he directs his life despite biological or sociological influences. Few fall at either extreme. Most people are a mixture but gravitate in one direction or the other.

So, let us discuss the people who fall between these extremes. It makes for interesting beliefs and behavior. For example, many believe in the "it was his time to go" philosophy exercise daily. Why? If one believes nothing he does will affect the time when he will die, then why spend time exercising? Eat anything wanted and laze around on the couch. One may argue that he exercises to be healthier, even though it does not prolong his life. It is very strange logic to me.

If one believes nothing he does affects when he dies, why not drive 120 mph when no law-enforcement agency is around? I know of a police officer who would drive recklessly at breakneck speed with total disregard for safety. When questioned, he responded, "If it's my time, I will go; if not, I won't."

Many students have come to me and said they were meant to be addiction counselors because it is what God chose for them. That suggests that God chose some to be drunkards and drug addicts so that this person could counsel them. The logic is strange to me.

For many people, it is easier to believe in fate than the onus on us to help ourselves. It's mentally and physically lazier to believe in fate. I think God helps those who help themselves. Notice that helping oneself comes first. Where do you fall on this continuum?

When Does Behavior Become A Sin?

Article #50
The News Courier, June 27, 2008

Can a certain behavior be a sin in one century but not the next? Is a behavior a sin if you were raised to believe that it is not a sin? I was taught as a child that the age of "accountability" was twelve. But again, at what age, if any, are you accountable for a "sin" if you have been taught it is not a sin? We should distinguish between not knowing a behavior is a sin and being taught that a certain behavior is not a sin.

I do not claim to speak for God; I write about those who claim to speak for Him or those who create the doctrines and dogma of the different denominations and faiths at various historical moments. Many denominations in the Christian church teach a paradox about when one goes to heaven.

A few years ago, this was aptly demonstrated at a funeral I attended. The minister said that Jim, the deceased, was now in heaven. Five minutes later, the minister said Jim would go to heaven "at the second coming of Christ." To be honest, I do not think the minister was aware of the paradox.

For the sake of argument, let us use Saint Peter as the guardian of entry into the gates of heaven. There may very well be a large gatehouse at those pearly gates where countless "moral yardsticks" are stored. The fairer Saint Peter is to those who try to enter, the more complicated the judgment process and the greater the need for moral yardsticks. However, the simpler the process, the more unfair it will be; thus, it will require very few yardsticks.

Referring to the funeral I attended, let us go with "judgment day" as occurring on the second coming. As Paul writes in 1 Corinthians 15:13, "If there is no resurrection of the dead, then not even Christ has been raised." In Acts 17:31, "For he has set a day when he will judge the world with justice...."

You may wonder why I write about the need for multiple moral yardsticks if judgment day is to be fair but complicated. People are taught differently depending on when they are alive. Judging people who lived in different eras is complicated. Let us examine four situations:

- Same time/same belief: This is the easiest to judge. Two lived at the same time and believed the same about what behaviors are sinful. If Jim did not sin and Joe did, Jim would enter the gates, and Joe would not.
- Same time/different belief: We need additional measuring sticks. For instance, Jim has been taught that to enter the gates, one must be baptized, immersed underwater, to "wash away" his sins. On the other hand, Joe has been taught that "sprinkling" is all that's required. Are not two different measuring sticks needed?
- Different times/different beliefs: Take polygyny in the Mormon church and the marriage of Catholic priests. In the 1800s, polygyny was accepted in the Mormon church and thought to be ordained by God. By the 1900s, this belief was no longer accepted.

In the first several hundred years after Jesus died, Catholic priests were allowed to marry and have families. Marriage by priests has not been allowed for more than one thousand years because it is very "sinful." Thus, will Saint Peter not need four moral measuring sticks on judgment day? Two for the Mormon men who lived in two different centuries, both of whom were faithful to what they believed, and two for the Catholic priests who lived in different millenniums, both of whom were faithful to what they believed.

Another case in point regarding this third type concerns "acceptable grounds" for divorce in certain Protestant denominations. In another era, only adultery was acceptable. That is not the case now.

- Different times/same belief: Let's talk about tithing. In the Old Testament, tithing is required by faithful members. However, nowhere in the New Testament, which is the new covenant with God, is tithing required or even mentioned. Suppose two people appear before Peter on judgment day. One lived before Jesus's teachings, and one afterward. Neither believed in tithing. Does Peter need two measuring sticks?

Can behavior be a sin in one century but not the next? Is a behavior a sin if you were raised to believe it is not? I believe that the fairer the judgment, the more complicated the process. May God bless Saint Peter.

What Has Happened to the American Dream?

Article #51
The News Courier, July 6, 2008

As we celebrate the July 4th weekend, a recent nationwide survey related that fewer people than in earlier eras believe in the American Dream. What has happened to the American Dream? Maybe we have slumbered too long or misunderstood the dream's original meaning.

In 1931, James Truslow Adams coined the term "American Dream." He wrote, "that dream of a land in which life should be better and richer and fuller for everyone, with opportunity for each according to ability or achievement."

We understood and embraced the first part of Adam's definition as a nation. Since 1931, almost everyone's life has been "...better and richer and fuller...." My paternal grandfather once told me that during the depression, there was a ten-year period when he did not see a $20 bill. Now all people see $20 bills. It is the last part of Adam's definition— "...with opportunity for each according to ability or achievement"—that, in my opinion, America misconstrued.

We as a nation pride ourselves on being a land of equal opportunity. But equal opportunity does NOT mean equal outcome. We have misconstrued the American Dream as creating a land of equal outcomes. That is not in Adam's definition, nor should it be.

I believe there are three different societies regarding the relationships between opportunity and ability. Currently, which of the following do you think describes America:

SOCIETY A— "Equal treatment for equal ability"—This is the best society. Those who have equal abilities are treated equally. They have an equal chance for employment in a job, an equal chance for advancement in that job, and an equal chance to succeed and achieve.

SOCIETY B— "Unequal treatment for equal ability"—This is a prejudiced society. For approximately the last fifty years, this is the type of society America has tried not to be. We now have myriad laws, regulations, and government offices that try to prevent this. We have striven to be a Type A society, but in so doing, we may have created the next kind of society, Type C.

SOCIETY C—"Equal treatment for unequal ability"—This is an unfair society. People are treated the same but have different abilities. It is a society in which "no child is left behind;" a society in which advancement is not based on ability or lack thereof. Think for a moment; if no one can be left behind, then no one can be ahead. You can only not be behind if no one is ahead of you. It is a society that tries to create equal outcomes versus one that creates equal opportunities.

Therefore, returning to Adam's definition of the "American Dream," has America misconstrued the land of "…opportunity for each notwithstanding ability or achievement"? Concerning the concept of "no one left behind,' as Lao Tzu once wrote, "Truthful words are not beautiful. Beautiful words are not truthful.

In Academia, There Are Four Kinds of Students

Article #52
The News Courier, August 17, 2008

As the new academic year starts across America, allow an old college professor with more than thirty years of experience mentally meander about the kinds of students he has taught. There are four kinds of students, and I have taught them all.

Regarding learning, there are two important traits: aptitude and attitude. Aptitude is the capability and competence to learn and master concepts and skills. Attitude is the desire and drive to learn and master concepts or skills. Which is more important?

Truly gifted students have both traits. They have the innate intelligence to understand concepts and a powerful passion for mastering them. They want to thrive and triumph and make the world a better place. As a teacher, these students are the ones you love to have in class because they are the most likely to improve the world. As we say in the teaching profession, "They keep you on your toes." I love being on my toes.

The second kind of student has the attitude but not the aptitude. They have the yearning, enthusiasm, and passion for learning but do not have much innate comprehension. These students sweat. They work hard, do their homework, and dream of a better life for themselves and the world. Many succeed. These students are a joy to teach. As Thomas Edison once said, "Genius is 99 percent perspiration and 1 percent inspiration."

The third kind of student is the most frustrating. This student disappoints the education system. This student can succeed but does not have the interest. The second type of student does not have the innate ability but has passion; this third type has the ability but does not care to learn. These students are challenging because they are mentally lazy. As the saying goes, "A mind is a terrible thing to waste," but a good mind is more terrible if squandered.

Finally, the fourth and last student should not be in college. Many will disagree with me. As Lao Tsu said, "Truthful words are not beautiful." College is not for everyone. These students occupy seats and pay tuition. These are the students who have neither the aptitude nor attitude and yet want a college degree. Sometimes they think they deserve it. The educational system has placated them, not educated them. Higher education in the United States has become more about economics than academics.

Early in my teaching career, I overheard a seasoned professor remark that he taught one in a class of twenty-five students, and the other 24 were there to support the system. I disagree strongly with his rationale. Many more of the twenty-five can be taught, but some simply support the system.

In conclusion, I hope to have the first kind of student in my class, those with aptitude and attitude. But if I had to choose between a student who is determined but has a Volkswagen mind versus one with a Cadillac mind but too lazy to put fuel in it, give me the Volkswagen. I will put a coat of wax on it and make it shine as much as possible.

Advance Beyond Your Opinion: The Three Stages of Learning

Article #53
The News Courier, September 14, 2008

If we do not continually learn, the mind narrows and slowly dies. Some learning is easy. Some learning is difficult. Some learning is a joy, and some is not. In my opinion, there are three stages of learning.

The first stage of learning is childlike. You form an opinion or belief about an issue or concept. You then can say, "I know!" This first stage is a joy and is easy.

The second stage becomes more difficult. It is when you realize that the opinion or belief you had earlier formed is not necessarily true. As Artemis Ward once said, "It ain't so much the things we don't know that get us into trouble. It's the things we know that just ain't so!" But how do we come to this realization? Mostly, I think it is by listening to or reading information with which we do not agree! Think for a moment; how much do you learn if you only listen to or read opinions and beliefs with which you agree? All you do is confirm what you think, a process known as confirmatory bias or selective perception. The mind does not grow. The mind is like a rubber band; once it is stretched, it cannot return to its original shape. If it is never stretched, it remains the same.

Recently I was reading a book. I disagreed with several statements. I wanted to put the book down. I kept reading, however, because I knew that was the only way I would learn. I was successful. When I finished the book, I had a new and different perspective. Instead of, "I know," I said, "I know that I do not know." Again, such learning can be hard, but it can stretch the rubber band.

I tell the students in my Critical Thinking class that I hope they know less when they complete the course than they did when it began. Many succeed. Some do not; they are the ones that have their minds made up.

As a young college student, I was in class one day, listening to one of the most learned men I had ever known. He made a statement that blew me away.

I faced a dilemma and three options: First, I could reject what he said; second, I could reject what I had previously learned; or I could go on a personal journey, study both sides, and reach a conclusion. I chose the third option and have been thankful ever since.

Many people ask me what I appreciate the most about my education. The two things I appreciate the most are a comfortable lifestyle and the fact that it freed my mind.

The third stage of learning is when you realize, "I know that no one knows." You realize no one's opinion or belief is entirely correct. Is this not the beginning of wisdom? Socrates taught that we come to true knowledge by recognizing our lack of knowledge. Does not this third stage encourage more understanding and tolerance of other people and their opinions?

No longer must it be "my way or the highway." Instead, we learn that the highway runs in both directions. If we drive in opposite directions, we become farther apart. If we drive toward each other, we can meet in the middle to talk.

I believe many of the world's problems result from people never advancing beyond the first stage of thinking. For many, it must be their way and only their way. They only read and listen to what they already believe. Some learning is difficult. If we do not continually learn, the mind narrows and slowly dies.

Get Out and Vote Tuesday–No $50 Jackass Needed Here

Article #54
The News Courier, November 2, 2008

All Americans couldn't always vote. Originally, one had to own land, be the right skin color, and be the right gender. There was no "universal suffrage" (universal voting). Doesn't seem democratic, does it?

But wait. Did the Founding Fathers want a democratic government? Maybe they wanted a republic, not a democracy controlled by mass suffrage. Believe it or not, the Constitution, drafted in 1787, did not specifically grant anyone voting rights. Alexander Keyssar, in *The Right to Vote*, notes that only Section 2 of Article 1 speaks to elections to the House of Representatives. Section 1 of Article 2 relates that each state could decide how the presidential electors would be chosen. Article 4 reads vaguely that the federal government was to "guarantee to every state in this Union a Republican Form of Government." Voting rights were not mentioned.

In colonial America, Benjamin Franklin wrote: "Today a man owns a jackass worth fifty dollars, and he is entitled to vote, but before the next election, the jackass dies; the jackass is dead, and the man cannot vote. Now gentlemen, pray inform me, in whom is the right of suffrage? In the man or the jackass?" In colonial America, a white man had to own property worth fifty dollars to vote in some places. A woman could own a barn full of jackasses and could not vote. A black man could own a whole pasture full of jackasses and could not vote. Doesn't seem democratic, does it? But again, did the Founding Fathers want a true democracy?

This Tuesday, November 4, 221 years after the Constitution was written, there will be universal adult voting because of a slow process of specific voting rights. The history of those specific rights varies from state to state. In 1844, New York dropped its property ownership requirement, but in 1846 said, it only applied to white men. Massachusetts dropped its property requirement in 1821; Virginia dropped its in 1850, and so it went from state to state, each dropping the requirement.

Only white men could vote until the late 1860s. With the passage of the thirteenth, fourteenth, and fifteenth amendments to the Constitution, black men could legally vote. In reality, however, many could not vote because of myriad restrictions. These restrictions would not be removed until the 1960s.

Even when the US Constitution allowed black men to legally vote in the 1860s, the Constitution did not allow a woman of any color to vote. Women could not vote in all American states until 1920.

Like many states, Alabama has a checkered history concerning voting rights. In 1819 you had to be a white male, have lived in the state for one year, and be a US citizen. In 1875 the state Constitution was amended to say, "No education qualification for suffrage...shall be made by law." That was amended in 1901 when a voter had to be able to "read or write any article of the Constitution of the United States in the English language." The man was exempt from the literacy requirement if he owned forty acres of land or real estate assessed at $300. Also, in 1901, the male had to pay a poll tax of $1.50 for those aged 21 to 45.

The Republic of the USA is slowly becoming more and more democratic, not less as many think. So, Tuesday, November 4, 2008, is a historic election. In the process of this presidential election, a woman almost secured her party's nomination. In contrast, a man half black and half white did secure that party's nomination. Go vote, dear reader, and you don't even have to own a $50 jackass!

The God of Credit

Article #55
The News Courier, December 14, 2008

The world is in economic chaos. Maybe what "caused" it was a shrinking third, wood, and a piece of cardboard. Sounds crazy? Let me explain, but first, let me warn the reader; I am a psychologist, not an economist. I do have, however, a degree in business. I got it after I came to Athens State while teaching full-time. Why? Well, the more I studied human behavior, the more I realized it revolves around the dollar bill. I still believe that. But let us return to the shrinking third, wood and the piece of cardboard.

I believe easy access to credit for millions is now "causing" billions of dollars to be given away. In my Critical Thinking class, I teach that we rarely truly know the exact cause of an event. We can study the triggering factors and the contributing factors. Thus, the shrinking third, wood and the cardboard piece, fall into these categories. What ties all three "causes" together? The god of credit.

Approximately 3,000 years ago, credit was born in Assyria, Egypt, and Babylon. In the fourteenth century, the bill of exchange was created, and this type of bill eventually became the banknote. Originally the buyer had to pay one-third of the purchase cost, and the other two-thirds were promised by this bill of exchange. This 33 percent one had to pay became 20 percent, 10 percent, and eventually zero percent. In recent years, people could buy homes with no money down and even borrow the loan's closing costs. Thus, people borrowed 105 percent of the cost of their house. The one-third cost that had to be paid upfront became less than zero. The third shrank and shrank.

Now, wood became a contributing factor. In 1730, Christopher Thompson, a merchant of wood furniture, was the first to advertise that his furniture could be bought on credit. The buyer could make regular weekly payments. These days, there are furniture ads in which one can purchase furniture with no money down and no payments for a year. Credit has come a long way.

Moreover, credit wood for extending credit in another form. From the eighteenth century to the early twentieth-century, "tallymen" became popular. These men sold clothes to people who could pay for them in small weekly payments. They kept a "tally" on a wooden stick. On one side was notched the amount of debt, and on the other side was a record of the payments.

Thus, now people could buy furniture and clothes on credit but not dinners. That would have to wait until 1950. The Diners Club card resulted from a change of clothing and a forgotten wallet. In 1949, Frank McNamara had a business meeting at a local restaurant. Before going, he changed his suit but left his wallet in the old one. This spurred McNamara, along with his business associate Ralph Schneider, to creatively produce a diner's card made of cardboard. And the rest is history.

Wood and cardboard were early prophets for the god of plastic. We are now living in economic chaos. Chaos occurs when people who cannot handle money are continually handed plastic credit cards.

Manipulative Cupid Computer Causes Relationship Problems

Article #56
The News Courier, December 21, 2008

There is new cancer among us. It has devastated many families, causing heartache for children and heartbreak for adults. It is neither a cancer of the body nor the brain but of the flesh and the mind. The disease is caused neither by viral nor bacteria but by a manipulative machine—the Cupid computer.

This week, a former student told me his wife had left him after ten years of marriage to live with a man in Kentucky. She had met him through the computer. The student had married the young lady even though she had a three-month-old baby with another man. He is the only father the young lad knows. The woman left in the night, leaving her husband and child. I am sure the man in Kentucky did not want the boy. This boy, who had been well-behaved, now has behavioral problems. His behavior is understandable; his mother's behavior is not. This cancer has ruined his Christmas.

My first personal experience with this cancer was several years ago. It involved one of my renters. One month, the rent was several days late. I went to the house to check into the matter. Upon arriving, the young man met me at the door and told me he and his wife were getting a divorce. I was dumbfounded because this couple always seemed very much in love. They had two daughters, about fourteen and eight. He shared that his wife was leaving him, taking the oldest daughter, and flying to Australia to be with a man she had met online and never in person. The man in Australia did not want the youngest daughter. The wife sold their furniture to help pay for two one-way airline tickets.

At the airport, the youngest daughter cried and begged her mother to take her. She didn't. Later the child would say, "I am very sad. My heart aches." Within a month, the woman's husband left Athens, with his youngest daughter in tow, to live with a woman in Wisconsin. He had never met her in person, either. The young daughter's heartache was understandable; her parents' behavior was not.

Last week, I discussed this new cancer with one of my colleagues. In addition to teaching, he is also a minister. He related a similar situation that occurred in his church. One of his parishioners left his three children and wife for a woman in New Jersey. Who introduced them? The Cupid computer. The young man has returned to North Alabama, and his personal life is in ruins. His former wife will not take him back. Her behavior is understandable; his behavior is not. Their children's Christmas has been ruined.

How can society find a cure for this social cancer? How can families prevent future outbreaks of adult heartbreak and children's heartache? How can we quarantine this manipulative machine, the Cupid computer?

As with any social disease, it will take willpower. In many marriages, mates gradually lose their attraction and appreciation for each other. Many adults seek romance and the novelty of a new person. The "in love" feeling is caused by brain chemistry. The surging brain chemicals may be caused indirectly by the anonymity of the computer. Anonymity spawns bravado. People write things on a computer they would never say in public. Wanton words lead to sexy sentences. Sexy sentences lead to lustful love. Lustful love leads to fractured families.

The heartaches and ruined Christmases of innocent children are not worth the momentary surge of brain chemicals. There is new cancer among us.

Are Lives Considered Equal When American Lives Are at Stake?

Article #57
The News Courier, January 25, 2009

Are lives equal?

President Obama, whom I admire greatly, stated in his inaugural address: "As for our common defense, we reject as false the choice between our safety and our ideals… Those ideals still light the world, and we will not give them up for expedience's sake. And so, to all other peoples and governments who are watching today…know that America is a friend of each nation and every man, woman, and child who seeks a future of peace."

Is every life in every nation equal?

President Obama's speech brought to mind a class project I created at Athens State University. Every semester I post the following scenario to my Critical Thinking class. The scenario is that the US military has intervened in a foreign country to restore peace. What is an acceptable ratio of American soldiers' deaths and foreign civilians? Is a rate of one-to-one acceptable? Is it okay for one soldier to die to save one foreign life?

Or, for every American soldier's death, should five foreign civilians be saved? Is it 1:10?

The students' responses ran the gamut.

One wrote: "I don't think any American lives should be lost at the cost of saving foreign people…."

A classmate offered a similar opinion. He wrote: "The only condition that could justify the loss of American lives is the direct threat to the freedoms and liberties of our country and its inhabitants."

On the other end of the continuum of thought, a student answered, "Let us not measure human's lives by them being American or foreign… Many Americans value their lives at a higher price than a foreign stranger's. Let us be equal."

Some could not find an acceptable ratio, an "expedient rate," if you will. I could see the helpless dismay on their faces as they tried to write.

Some students did find an acceptable ratio.

One penned, "I propose that a ratio of one to fifty be imposed when evaluating a warfare situation. If American lives are going to be sacrificed, it should make a large impact."

Another offered, "I think that pushing for a high but realistic ratio is for every one solder's death at least twenty-five foreign civilians should be saved."

A very thoughtful student responded this way: "If I say one American life can be taken so five foreign lives can be saved, I would be wrong. If that one American life was my spouse, father, mother, or sister, then it is nowhere near an adequate ratio. On the other hand, if I were a foreigner, and five of my family members were saved, and one American was killed, then it would be adequate."

If lives are equal, will America be a friend of each nation and every man, woman, and child who seeks peace? Or will America be a better friend if there is oil in that nation?

In this case, lives are equal, but some are more equal than others.

What do you think is an acceptable death rate for American soldiers?

An Admitted Wrong as Compared to an Amended Wrong

Article #58
The News Courier, February 8, 2009

In my opinion, there are different kinds of "sin." Let us discuss, in particular, that type of sin against other people, where one has hurt other individuals. Much has been written about forgiveness of these sins through "grace;" very little has been written about reparation of these types of sins. Reparation means the righting of a wrong, making amends to the victim. Reparation is returning to the person what one has taken from him.

I believe there are four kinds of sinners when it comes to reparation. In my opinion, the first and most forgiven individual is one who asks for God's forgiveness and amends the wrong done to the victim. In my opinion, God smiles on this person.

The second individual is the least forgiven, if forgiven at all. This is the sinner who seeks repentance neither from God nor the victim. This person is self-centered and has a "devil may care" attitude. This behavior, at its extreme, is psychopathic.

I would like to discuss the other two types of sinners further. Of the two, who does God smile on the most? Which one has repented the most?

After sinning for a day, a week, a month, or a lifetime, the third sinner seeks repentance and asks God for forgiveness but does not right the wrong with the victim. If money has been stolen, none is returned; if lives have been shattered, he ignores the broken pieces and walks away. This individual was not there for his children, asks God for forgiveness, and is still not there for them when they become adults.

Do we not, as parents, upon learning our child wronged another child, instruct our child to "Go and tell him you are sorry." Does not God expect the same from His children?

The belief that one can be forgiven for offenses without giving back to the offended party may stem from Romans 3:24, which says one is justified "freely" by grace. Of the four gospels in the New International Version (NIV) of the New Testament, there is no mention of "grace" in Mark, the earliest Gospel, nor in Matthew, the Jewish Gospel. Grace is mentioned once in Luke; and four times in John, all in the first chapter. Of the four references in John, the English word "grace" substitutes for three slightly different Greek words, which likely have slightly different connotations. In the letters of Paul," grace" is mentioned around 100 times in one of its three Greek versions.

The fourth and final type of sinner is the person who seeks forgiveness from the victim but never formally asks God for forgiveness. The reader may argue that such a person does not exist. But they do; even some agnostics and atheists make amends. And some believe in God but neither attend church nor ask for repentance on Sunday but make amends Monday through Saturday. They try to the best of their ability to glue back the shattered pieces of the family vase they have broken.

I have heard people claim "grace" made them complete, but they have forgotten about their victims. Some have boasted they did not need to seek anyone else's forgiveness.

Of the last two types, who does God respect the most; the one who has admitted the wrong or the one who has amended the wrong? Can one be commendable to God without first being amendable to his fellow man?

Just How Religious Is Alabama?

Article #59
The News Courier, February 14, 2009

I read the February 7 issue of *The Decatur Daily*, "How Religious Are You? Gallup Poll confirms it—Alabama is highly religious, and Vermont is not—but why?" The story reminded me of Francis Bacon's claim that "Man prefers to believe what he prefers to be true."

I argue that if one judges a state's religiosity by its behavior (its "walk," not its "talk"), then Vermont is much more religious than Alabama.

Please understand I am as Southern as one can get; I was born and reared in the South and attended schools in four Southern states. We in the South, however, do not walk our religion as well as we talk about it. I offer the following as food for critical thought, not criticism.

Let's compare Alabama to Vermont because that was the case in the previous article. This comparison will be done by the rate of certain behaviors per 100,000 population in both states, according to the 17th edition of "State Rankings," a reference book published by Morgan Quitno.

An individual is twice as likely to get murdered in Alabama compared to Vermont. Our state ranks eighteenth, while Vermont ranks thirty-fourth.

Moreover, a woman is more apt to be raped in Alabama than in Vermont. Alabama ranks eighteenth in this category, while Vermont comes in forty-first.

Alarmingly, an individual is eleven times more likely to be robbed in Alabama than in Vermont. Concerning aggravated assault, one is three times more likely to be assaulted in Alabama.

Alabama's property crime rate is almost double Vermont's. Likewise, an individual is almost twice as likely to be burglarized in our Southern state.

On other personal issues, an Alabamian is three times more likely to file personal bankruptcy than a Vermonter. If one is religious, shouldn't he pay what he owes his fellow man? After all, the Golden Rule and Romans 13:8 suggest as much.

If a person is religious, should they not be less likely to divorce? The divorce rate is higher in Alabama than in that northern state. Alabama ranks fourth in the nation on divorce, while Vermont ranks twenty-first.

Moreover, more babies are born to unmarried women in Alabama than in Vermont. Alabama is above the national average on this issue; Vermont is below it.

Living in Alabama makes the risk of getting AIDS seven times more likely than in Vermont.

In Alabama, one is more likely to be murdered, raped, assaulted, robbed, have a child out of wedlock, file bankruptcy, be divorced, and get AIDS than someone living in Vermont. So just how religious is Alabama?

Recalling Bacon's words, maybe Alabama prefers to believe what Alabama prefers to be true.

Maggots, Mortgage Loans, Dog Poop, and a Dodge Truck

Article #60
The News Courier, February 22, 2009

The nation is currently trying to dodge a depression. I am currently driving a Dodge truck that is eleven years old. One of the stimulus proposals is to lower the mortgage interest rate for people who have had difficulty paying their home mortgage loans. I have neither read nor heard any proposal on lowering interest rates for people who have punctually met their monthly mortgage obligations.

Please understand that I have no problem assisting people who have tried to help themselves and cannot meet their financial obligations due to circumstances beyond their control. But should we help those who did not meet their financial obligations when the circumstances were under their control? Many people whose mortgage payments are reduced will not drive eleven-year-old vehicles.

My family and I have been blessed in ways that are beyond what I personally deserve. Tracy and I own rental houses, and we have had excellent tenants for the most part. For the most part, but we have had a few renters who left the house very unclean.

At different times, I have removed maggots from a freezer, a refrigerator, and a crockpot left on the stove. I have cleaned pennies intermingled with dog poop in a shed behind one of my houses. (My father told me as a boy never to be too good to pick up a penny, so to this day, I pick up all lost pennies). Moreover, I have cleaned up other people's body hair left in the bathrooms. You get the gist of what I deal with as a landlord.

I know of former tenants who moved out owing me money and left the rental house unclean while they moved into their new house purchased with a sub-prime loan. By now, they may be having trouble paying their mortgage loan. If I understand this correctly, their interest rate may be lowered while I, cleaner of dog poop, certain body hairs, and maggots, and on-time payer of my mortgage payments, will see no decrease in the interest rates I pay on the rental house they left without cleaning.

My parents told me that "hard work never hurt anybody," which is true. Sadly, these days, it's more accurate to say, "hard work never hurt anybody, but you may pay higher interest on loans." To be clear, I do not begrudge anyone paying lower interest on loans. But shouldn't those who have always paid on time qualify for a lower interest rate? Why penalize good financial management?

This country became great because of people who used their hands to help themselves and lived by the Golden Rule; it was not built by people who expected a golden handout.

Meanwhile, the country is still trying to dodge a depression, and I am still driving that old Dodge truck and picking up pennies.

The Other Resurrections and The Descension Into Hell

Article #61
The News Courier, April 12, 2009

Today the Christian religion celebrates Easter, the resurrection of Christ on the third day after his crucifixion. The early church may have believed the Spirit of Jesus was active during his forty hours of burial. Remember, it was Jewish custom to count any part of a day as a whole day. Thus, the last part of Friday was the first day, Saturday was the second day, and the first part of Sunday was the third day. Thus, Jesus was buried for approximately forty hours.

This activity of Jesus's Spirit may be partly explained by an obscure passage in the Gospel of Matthew. It relates that Jesus was not the only one to be resurrected in the three days of Passover. In my entire life, I have neither heard a sermon nor read a Sunday school lesson about this passage.

The Gospel of Matthew 27: 51-53 records four events. After Jesus gave up the Spirit on that Friday, the first three instances were as follows. The curtain of the temple was torn in two from top to bottom. The earth shook, and the rocks split. The tombs broke open, and the bodies of many holy people were resurrected. Thus, according to the Bible, Jesus was not the only one resurrected. The fourth occurrence occurs after Jesus arose. Verse 53 relates that the risen holy people went into Jerusalem and appeared to many people. Strangely, these resurrected holy people were never heard from again in Matthew and are not, to the best of my knowledge, ever mentioned anywhere else in the entire New Testament. Why?

Why would the Gospel of Matthew author include this while the authors of the other gospels did not? Remember that Matthew is the most Jewish Gospel, and the Jewish community, the sect called the "way," which was the forerunner of Christianity, would have been familiar with the "Book of Enoch." Even though Enoch is not in the Bible, it was considered "scriptural" in this community. For example, verses 14 and 15 in the Letter of Jude in the New Testament are almost verbatim from Enoch. Most scholars date Enoch to the second century before Christ. Fragments of ten separate manuals of this book were found among the Dead Sea Scrolls at Qumran, thus predating Christ. Enoch is still read today in certain Coptic Christian churches in Ethiopia. Joseph B. Lumpkin, in *The Lost Book of Enoch,* writes, "there are over one hundred comments in the New Testament which finds precedence in the Book of Enoch."

Let me now quote from Enoch (Richard Laurence and R. H. Charles's translations) Chapter fifty-one, verses 1 and 2:

> *And in those days shall the earth also give back that which*
> *Has been entrusted to it, and Sheol (the grave) also shall give back*
> *That which it has received, and hell shall give back that which*
> *It owes. For in those days, the elect one shall arise, and he shall*
> *Choose the righteous and holy from among them. For the day*
> *Has drawn near that they should be saved.*

Thus, in my opinion, to fulfill Enoch's prophecy, Matthew writes of resurrections occurring in addition to the one of Christ.

Moreover, a question to be asked is what did the early church believe the Spirit of Jesus was doing during the approximate forty hours his body was buried? According to 1 Peter 3:18-20, He descended into hell. It reads in part, "...He was put to death in the body but made alive by the Spirit, through whom also he went and preached to the spirits in prison who disobeyed long ago when God waited patiently in the days of Noah while the ark was being built...." (NIV).

In addition, the Catholic Apostles Creed reads in part, "...Jesus Christ... born of the Virgin Mary, suffered under Pontius Pilate, was crucified, died, and buried; he descended into hell; the third day he rose again from the dead...." Many Protestant churches, however, have omitted the phrase "he descended into hell" from their Apostles Creed.

The belief that He descended into hell was necessary again, in my opinion, to fulfill Enoch's prophecy in chapter 51 "...hell shall give back that which it owes...the Elect One shall rise, and he shall choose the righteous and holy from among them." And thus, Matthew writes, "The tombs broke open, and the bodies of many holy people who had died were raised to life."

Today the Christian religion celebrates Easter, the resurrection of Christ on the third day after his crucifixion. But we do not celebrate, as the early church did, his activities during those three days.

Ignorance About Medicine Risks Dying

Article #62
The News Courier, May 17, 2009

Understanding the risk of living and dying is very important. That is why most people take medicine, is it not? Let me offer you three scenarios, and in which one would you most likely agree to take medicine?

RISK 1: Taking a particular medicine can reduce your risk of dying by just nine-tenths of 1 percent.

RISK 2: Taking this medicine reduces your risk of dying by 22 percent.

RISK 3: 111 people must take this medicine to save just one life.

Again, of the above three medicines, which one would you be most likely to take to reduce your risk of dying? Most of you will choose the second scenario. But in all three risk situations, it is the same medicine.

Thus, one must understand the risk of ignorance regarding drugs. The drug is Pravastatin, a cholesterol-lowering drug. Data can be presented in different ways. Usually, the "presenter" will choose the method that "proves" his viewpoint. Usually, the "presenter" is the pharmaceutical company.

Risk 1 is termed the "absolute risk reduction" and is the proportion of patients who die without treatment (they take a placebo which is a fake non-medicinal pill) minus those who die with treatment (they take the drug). The space allotted for this column does not allow me to do the mathematical analysis for each scenario. I will offer a verbal definition of each.

Risk 2 is called the "relative risk reduction" and is found by taking the number found in the "Absolute risk reduction" and dividing that number by the proportion of patients who die without the treatment (the placebo).

Risk 3 is entitled the "number needed to treat" and is the number of people who must participate in the treatment to save just one life. As you can imagine, most drug companies use the data presented in the Risk 2 scenario because it puts them "in the best light."

Another vivid example of this was recently reported in the *USA TODAY* newspaper of a study published in the New England Journal of Medicine. A European study examined the beneficial effects of screening for prostate cancer. It reported that screening reduced the risk of prostate cancer by about 20 percent (the relative risk reduction), sounds pretty good. The journal and newspaper, to their credit, reported that 1,000 men would have to be screened for ten years to save just one life (number needed to treat). That doesn't sound nearly as good.

Again, when one listens to drug commercials on television and radio or reads about them in magazines and newspapers, the advertisements present the medicine positively, the relative risk reduction. We are encouraged to take them to reduce our risk of dying. We should ask how effectively it reduces our risk, the absolute risk reduction, and how many must be treated.

Recently, after my annual physical examination, my physician and I discussed the merits of taking a cholesterol-reducing drug (a different one from Pravastatin). After he gave me the number needed to treat to save one life, I chose not to take the medicine. He agreed with my decision.

Understanding the risk of living and dying is important.

Source: Calculated Risks, How to Know When Numbers Deceive You by Gerd Gigerenzer.

Two Mules, A Tractor, Texting, and Tweeting

Article #63
The News Courier, July 5, 2009

When I was young, I thought Pa was backward. Now, at age fifty-nine, I know, at age fifty-nine, how my maternal grandfather felt when he was the same age. The older I get, the smarter he seems.

Pa (Lem) Hatchett never drove a tractor. Instead, he drove two mules. He needed no diesel, oil, mechanic, or manual; only hay and water, and the mules even helped him harvest the hay. Pa thought mules were easier to handle than a tractor, and he did not want to learn how to use a tractor. He could haul square-baled hay by himself, stand on the ground, and use certain voice commands; the two mules would go, turn right, turn left, or stop. When driving a tractor, it isn't easy to haul square-baled hay by yourself. Sometimes less is more and easier.

I recently told my wife I wanted a simple television with a remote. I got a tv, disk player, and stereo with three remote controls. I counted over 150 buttons; I must ask my nine-year-old son for help. When I was nine, I thought my Pa wasn't hip. When a man realizes his ancestors were right, he has a son who thinks his father is wrong.

I grew up with a television that had only three channels. Occasionally, my brother or I would have to scamper on top of the house to turn the antenna for better reception. But I watched more complete shows then than I do now while "channel surfing" with seventy-three channels. Sometimes more is less and frustrating.

In *Distracted: The Erosion of Attention and the Coming Dark Age*, Maggie Jackson claimed we are inundated with emails, text messages, tweets, and phone calls. According to the Nielson Company, in the last quarter of 2008, the average American teenager sends eighty texts daily on iPods and cellphones. In school, teenagers are becoming so adept at texting they can do it in their purse, pocket, or underneath the desk while "listening" to the instructor. Whereas all these instant technological advances were supposed to attract connections, they may also create a distracted generation that cannot communicate effectively face-to-face.

Moreover, a survey done by Harris Interactive on 655 teens aged thirteen to eighteen found that one in five of this age group has "sexted." Sexted means the teenager has sent or received sexually suggestive texts via their email or cellphones. This behavior makes them vulnerable to sexual predators, yet they continue to do it. Sometimes more is more and risky.

According to the Pew Internet and American Life project done in December 2008, 75 percent of young people use online social media, such as Facebook or Twitter, while only 19 percent of those aged forty-five to fifty-four, 10 percent aged fifty-five to sixty-four, and only 7 percent of those over age sixty-five. I have never used Facebook or Twitter, and, like Pa, I do not want to learn how. I thought tweeting was something birds do, and besides, Pa's mules are looking better every day. Sometimes less is less.... and simpler.

We Grow Up by Learning to Move Upward

Article #64
The News Courier, August 23, 2009

Today I will write with my psychology pen. I write about an emotion, a feeling, for which the English language has no word, but the German language does. The German language is so much richer in its expressions. As a student of it for two years at the collegiate level, I found it difficult but very educational.

This emotion has different levels, and each of you has experienced them. Some of these experiences, the overt ones you admit to, and the others, the covert ones, you will never admit.

The German word is "schadenfreude," meaning you wish someone bad fortune or failure. The overt or open experiences of this are the ones you are willing to admit. For one example, it happens every Saturday afternoon in the fall. Rabid Alabama fans always hope Auburn loses; passionate Auburn fans wish for failure for Alabama. Many people openly express schadenfreude toward Notre Dame on autumn Saturday afternoons. I have heard different people say they are for any team that plays against this Catholic university.

This first form of schadenfreude, for the most part, is harmless. The other type, the covert or hidden form, may not be. This second type happens everywhere to everyone but is admitted by no one. It occurs in families, work settings, politics, athletics, religion, and other places too numerous to mention.

In families with grown children, if one is very successful, the other children may wish the prosperous one were less so, but they will never admit it. To his face, they may even wish him greater success but will never let it be known they privately wish he would fail.

In work settings, there is usually a 'star' of the corporation or business who is quite successful. The other workers may wish this star would come crashing to the ground, but they will never admit it.

In politics, there are rabid Republicans who silently hope that every initiative on President Obama's agenda will fail. Moreover, stanch Democrats during the last administration quietly wished the Bush proposals ill luck. In neither case would they admit it.

In athletics, hoping the team you are playing against fails is acceptable. But it is a different matter if you, as a second-teamer, wish the person who plays on your team's first squad at your position falls and breaks his leg. We admit the first but never the second.

In religion, it may be harmless to wish Notre Dame or Brigham Young University bad fortune on the playing field. However, it is a different situation to hope for the demise of the Catholic faith or the Mormon religion. Yet many evangelical Protestants do so – but they will not admit it. Their schadenfreude, too, is silent—it doesn't sound too Christlike, and it goes against the Golden Rule.

I have written all the above to write the following. Wishing failure to a person or any entity more successful than you does not make you a larger person; it makes you a smaller one. We only grow when we move upward—not when someone beside us is cut down. This hidden type of schadenfreude is probably a natural human emotion. However, knowing that should inspire us to work harder to succeed rather than wishing for others to fail.

Can There Be Different Kinds of Truth?

Article #65
The News Courier, September 27, 2009

"How much reality must we choose to ignore for the greater good of our own souls and society?" Rod Dreher asked this question recently in an article in a national newspaper, *USA Today*.

The article was entitled "How much 'truth' is too much truth?" He also quoted the belief Jesus espouses in the Bible, "You shall know the truth, and the truth shall set you free." At one point in the article, he admits he is conflicted about the matter.

Does knowing the truth always set you free? I, too, am conflicted about the answer. I believe and teach that we should always seek the truth, wherever it may lead.

Understand that I define "truth" as what has happened in the past and is happening in the present. What I wish to have happened or wish were happening is not the truth. Sometimes knowing the truth, however, makes one's life more miserable. For example, a child truly loves her father, truly loves him as a teenager, and then learns as an adult that he is not her biological father. This begs the question, has the truth become too much truth? Later in life, however, when confronted with a severe illness, knowing this fact about her genetic heritage saves her life (sets her free). Thus, should one always seek the truth?

One should prepare if he searches for the truth to be able to accept that truth. Also, one should learn for which kind of truth to search. I believe there are three kinds of truth—the Beautiful Truth, the Ugly Truth, and the Wildflower Truth. First, there is the Beautiful Truth, the flower of truths. For example, when you truly love someone, and they truly love you in return. Then there is the Ugly Truth, the wild weed of truths, as in those marriages where neither spouse loves the other. Finally, there is the combination of ugly and beautiful, the Wildflower of truths, when you love someone, and they do not love you in return. Some may argue there is no Wildflower of truths, but there is. The Beautiful Truth is no one wants to grow old; the Ugly Truth is if you don't grow old, you won't. The Wildflower

134 | CAN THERE BE DIFFERENT KINDS OF TRUTH?

of truth is that as you add more years to your life—there is a decline in your physical and mental abilities.

Moreover, it is a Beautiful Truth to own land in America. At the same time, the Ugly Truth is that land was taken from the Native Americans. The Wildflower of this truth is that America eventually became a moral leader in the world based on a moral weakness in the beginning.

My twin adopted daughters are another example of the Wildflower of truth. Sydni and Sophi are little girls that have brought much Beautiful Truth (and activity) into our household. The Ugly Truth is that we "bought" the girls. When we adopted them, Tracy and I had $20,000 taped to our bodies to pass through customs at the airports. We "paid" the National Adoption Center in Kyiv, we "paid" the orphanage, we "paid" the judge, and the list continued. This was one of those times in my life when I thought the end justified the means.

Does knowing the truth always set you free? Just how much "truth" is too much truth?

Growing Wiser and Knowing Less
Part 1 of 2

Article #66
The News Courier, December 6, 2009

As one grows older, I believe one grows wiser. As one grows wiser, I believe one knows less.

And why would one know less if one is wiser? It is because of the connection between HIV, a radiator hose, smoking cigarettes, an inner tire tube, a light rain, and Janet Reno, the former Attorney General of the United States. Let me explain.

All of the above examples contribute to "cause." I believe "cause" is the most abused word in English. I have five college degrees, and I probably could put all that I know for a fact on the front and back of one single page of paper.

Every day one is inundated with what "causes" this situation or that situation. For instance, "the moral fabric of America is decaying because of …," Global warming is occurring because of …," or "America is mortgaging her future because of …" and the list goes on.

But let us get back to HIV. It cannot be said HIV singularly "causes" AIDS. Everyone who has had AIDS indeed had HIV. However, some people have had the virus and have never had AIDS. Thus, the virus cannot cause AIDS by itself.

Why some people can have the virus and not have the disease has intrigued scientists for years.

The virus is a necessary condition (the condition that must exist for the AIDS effect to occur). It is not the condition that will always produce AIDS.

And now, let us discuss the radiator hose. If one is driving a vehicle and a small pinhole occurs in the hose, and the person keeps driving, the engine will overheat. Thus, the pinhole, if the car is driven too long, is a sufficient condition enough to produce the heated engine effect, but it is not a necessary condition (again, a condition that must exist for the heated engine effect to occur). Other conditions can cause an overheated engine, such as a broken fan belt or too little coolant.

When one discovers a condition that is necessary and sufficient for an effect, one has truly found the cause of that effect. I know of very few conditions that are both necessary and sufficient. Thus, it takes fewer pages to write my wisdom.

Let us look at another issue—the relationship between smoking and lung cancer. It cannot be said that smoking "causes" lung cancer. Why? Because there are many people who have died of lung cancer and never smoked a day in their life. And there are many people who smoked their entire life and did not die of lung cancer (my grandfather Hatchett being one of them). Thus, smoking is neither necessary nor sufficient to cause lung cancer.

Remember a few years ago when Congress was investigating the major tobacco companies associated with the rising rates of lung cancer in America. The CEOs of the companies, lined up like dominos, were sitting before the congressional committee. Each was asked if smoking "caused" lung cancer, and each answered "no." They were correct. What they should have been asked is—"Does smoking contribute to lung cancer?"

"Contribute" is an especially important word when trying to establish causality.

Smoking and a boy on the inner tire tube have something in common, which will be addressed next week, along with Janet Reno and light rain.

Again, as one grows wiser, he knows less. Until next week...

Cause and Effect: On Growing Wiser and Knowing Less
Part 2 of 2

Article #67
The News Courier, December 13, 2009

Last week I addressed the concepts of necessary and sufficient conditions in trying to establish causality.

Today let us look at contributing conditions, unusual conditions, and triggering conditions as they relate to causality.

Let me use the following example to illustrate these. I am driving too fast on the highway while it is slightly raining. Realizing that I am driving too fast, I hit the brakes too hard, my vehicle slides off the road, and my car is damaged. What "caused" the accident?

The contributing factor was my speed. The unusual factor was that it was lightly raining. The triggering factor was my hitting the brakes. The triggering factor is the last condition that occurs before the effect, which in this case, is a wrecked vehicle.

Your response is probably, "so what"? I think hitting my brakes is why Albert Gore was not elected president in 2000, sort of. Let me explain.

If you remember, Gore lost the presidency since he lost the Electoral College vote and won the national popular vote. If Gore had won one more state in the popular vote, he would have had that state's Electoral College vote and, thus, the presidency. Also, recall he lost the state of Florida by the narrowest of margins in the popular vote. Do you remember all the recounts?

Why did he lose Florida? I think it is connected to a little boy floating into Florida on an innertube. His mother and others from Cuba had drowned at sea trying to reach our shores.

This little boy would eventually live with his mother's relatives. This floating child contributed to Gore's demise just like my speeding contributed to my accident.

Later, the little boy would be returned to Cuba to live with his father at the request of his father and the Cuban authorities. His return, however, came with a cost to Gore. Janet Reno, the former Attorney General under

Clinton, legally and forcefully took the boy from his maternal relatives. Taking the child by armed force was unusual, just like the light rain was the unusual situation in my automobile accident. Personally, I support Reno's action. If a man's son were in another country and the mother of that child had died, would not most men make every effort to get their son back?

Returning the child triggered an outrage among the Cuban American population in Florida and cost Gore enough votes to lose Florida and, thus, the Electoral College and the presidency. Therefore, the outrage and the hitting of my brakes, which triggered the automobile accident, are connected, sort of; both are the last factors before the effect.

Please understand I am not writing that the little boy floating in the ocean was the only single factor in Gore's loss. It could be argued that Clinton's affair with Monica Lewinsky cost Gore enough votes to doom his campaign; the list could go on and on. That is my point –there was no single "cause." As in life, there are very few single causes for the events we experience in everyday living. There are very few conditions that are both necessary and sufficient to cause the effect. As we grow older, we become wiser, and we know less.

Beware of Big Numbers: They're Usually Lies
Part 1 of 2

Article #68
The News Courier, February 7, 2010

Beware of big numbers! Big numbers are deceitful and misleading. People, organizations, and governments use them to sway your thinking. In this column and one next week, I would like to reveal the connection between Barbie dolls, coffee houses, euthanized animals, African women, brain cells, incarcerated Americans, and Warren Beatty's sex life. The connections, of course, are big numbers, and how they are all lies.

Let us begin with Warren Beatty's sex life. Peter Biskind published a book entitled "Star: How Warren Beatty Seduced America." The book was reviewed by *USA TODAY*. Biskind claims Warren Beatty has sexually conquered 12,775 women. It can't be true!

Warren Beatty is seventy-two years old. Let us say that by age eighteen, ol' Warren had bedded 275 women (a feat most teenage boys can only envy). If I subtract the eighteen years from Warren's present age, that leaves fifty-four years to conquer the remaining 12,500 women. If I multiply fifty-four years times 365 days per year, I get 19,710 days. Suppose I divide 12,500 women into those 19,710 days. In that case, ol' Warren has been bedding *a different woman every thirty-eight hours since age eighteen.* He may be prolific, but he is not that prolific.

Now to the claim made by PETA (People for the Ethical Treatment of Animals). Do not misunderstand; I am against animal cruelty, but even good organizations like PETA can use bad numbers. In the past, PETA has distributed information claiming the following: "This year, six to eight million animals will be killed every month in our nation's commercial, military, and federally funded university laboratories." That cannot be true.

Let us take the number seven million, half way between PETA's figure. Let it be argued that there are ten such laboratories in every state (there are not that many, but I always try to err in the claimant's favor). Since there are fifty states, there would be five hundred of these animal-killing labs in America. So if I divide seven million animals by 500 labs, the PETA organization claims that 14,000 animals are killed monthly in every lab. Now, if I divide that 14,000 by thirty days per month (note the animal killers are working all weekends), PETA claims that 467 animals are killed every day in every lab. Suppose I divide those 467 animals by eight work hours per day. In that case, PETA claims that fifty-eight animals are killed every working hour in every lab in America. That cannot be true.

Beware of big numbers; they are usually lies. Next week I will address incarcerated Americans, female genital mutilation of African women, Barbie dolls, and coffee shops. Until then...

Beware of Big Numbers, Usually Bunch Of Bull
Part 2 of 2

Article #69
The News Courier, February 14, 2010

Last week I addressed how large numbers lied about Warren Beatty's sex life and PETA's claim about the number of animals euthanized for scientific research. Today let us discuss Barbie dolls, coffee houses, incarcerated Americans, and genital mutilation of African women.

Let us begin with this female genital mutilation. In the past, printed information was distributed in a college class in northern Alabama about this procedure (it was not Athens State University). The material read female genital mutilation is the "cutting off or permanently destroying a woman's external sex organs." There are three types of this procedure: the Sunna, the clitoridectomy, and the infibulation. I do not want to discuss the difference between these operations. Instead, I want to discuss the number of women that supposedly have this procedure done to them yearly. The information said, "each year, 75 to 85 million African women are circumcised...." This big number can be debunked in one of two ways.

First, if I use Africa's population, 75 to 85 million women is an impossible number. The population of Africa is approximately one billion, half men and half women. One-half of one billion would be 500 million women. Therefore it would take only seven years to circumcise every female in Africa. Every female in Africa is not circumcised, and the practice has been occurring for many years.

Second, if I use the number of practitioners who perform this surgery, the claim falls flat. I talked to an expert about Africa. She said that, at the most, there are only one hundred "doctors" who perform this surgery in all of Africa.

If I multiply eight working hours per day times 365 days per year (notice, no "doctor" gets a single day off the entire year), I get a total of 2,920 hours. If I divide eighty million women by 2,920 hours, I get 27,397 girls per hour. Then if I divide 27,397 females by one hundred "doctors," I get a staggering 274 girls who have this operation each hour by each "doctor." Then divide

274 girls by sixty minutes; each doctor performs 4.55 operations per minute or one every thirteen seconds. That is impossible.

A different college textbook claims, "some two million African girls are mutilated each year." If it is only two million, every "doctor" performs this operation every eight minutes and forty seconds. Still impossible.

A few years ago, LIFE magazine predicted the number of Barbie dolls sold by 2091. The number was 208 quadrillion (a quadrillion has fifteen zeros). I did the math. The magazine claims that every person who has lived, is living now, and will have lived by 2091 will have owned 6,933,000 Barbie dolls. Can you picture a caveman sitting in his cave surrounded by his 6,933,000 Barbie dolls? Where do you put your seven million Barbie dolls?

LIFE magazine also predicted that in 2055, incarcerated Americans will number 126,153,000. Do the math. If the US population doubles in the next forty-five years, it means almost one in five Americans will be in prison. Whew!

Finally, the same LIFE edition predicted that there will be 13,067,000 coffee houses in America in fifteen years. According to the census, there are 19,354 "incorporated places" in the United States. So, if I divide 13,067,000 coffee houses by 19,354, each incorporated place in America will have 675 coffee houses. That's a lot of coffee and a lot of bull.

Beware of big numbers because they are usually a lot of bull.

Cut Taxes—Where Do We Cut Spending?

Article #70
The News Courier, April 25, 2010

I hear much about how the federal government should cut taxes. However, I hear very little about where the federal government should cut spending. Trust me, I do not like to pay taxes like most people, but I realize Uncle Sam, who has become Uncle Sugar to many, must collect money for the government to operate. I agree when I am told the U. S. government needs to balance its books. I then ask for suggestions on how the federal government should cut spending. I usually get blank stares, or I am offered the same old answers. In my opinion, the same old answers are not going to work.

Brian Riedl of The Heritage Foundation, a conservative think tank in Washington D. C., recently wrote about how Washington spends your tax money in 2010. He wrote that this year the federal government will spend $31,406 on each household in America but will only collect $18,276 in taxes from each household. Notice the $13,130 discrepancy between the numbers; this is each household's "deficit." I use the Heritage's calculations because I do not want to be attacked by the right that my numbers are "liberal."

I believe that Americans have trouble understanding the budget quandary because most people can't comprehend billions or trillions of dollars. So, I have taken the Heritage Foundation's numbers and put them on a scale of $100. Below is how the federal government spends that $100 on each household:

- Social Security/Medicare, $31.68
- Defense, $19.33
- Anti-poverty Programs, $17.40
- Unemployment Benefits, $5.22
- Interest on Federal Debt, $5.05
- Veteran's Benefits, $3.35
- Federal Employee Retirement Benefits (includes Veterans), $3.24

- Education (includes school lunches, special education programs, and college student financial aid), $2.91
- Highways/Mass transit, $1.95
- Health Research/ Regulation, $1.75
- Mortgage credit (Fannie Mae and Freddie Mac), $1.50
- All other programs (justice, international affairs, farm subsidies, social services, natural resources, energy, space exploration, environment, air transportation, and regional development) $6.62
- Total $100.00

Again, this $100 is what the federal government spends on each American household. But again the problem, however, is that this same government only collects $58.19 in taxes from each household. So how does the government pay the difference of $41.81? Simple, it borrows it.

As one can see, Social Security and Medicare amount to $31.68, almost one-third of the entire expenditures. Social Security is $19.07 of the $31.68, and Medicare costs the remaining $12.61. The average Social Security retirement benefit is now $1,117 per month. These will only grow larger unless they are reduced as the baby boomers move into this age category. The baby boomers, however, are the very people who kept these programs in the black in the past because of their sheer numbers. Social Security and Medicare are elephants in the room that no one wants to discuss, and the 800-pound gorillas in the same room that no one will confront.

It is hoped that if the U. S. can successfully exit both Iraq and Afghanistan, it could reduce the defense portion. According to the Center on Budget and Policy Priorities, the two wars account for $4.65 of the $19.33 of the defense budget.

The federal government MUST pay its interest of $5.05 on the federal debt. Thus, if I add the expenses for Social Security/Medicare plus defense plus the interest debt, it totals $56.06. Thus, after collecting $58.19 in taxes, it leaves a balance of $2.13.

Therefore, if taxes are not raised, and the federal government tries to balance its checkbook not to jeopardize future generations' prospects, $2.13 is all that is left to pay for EVERYTHING ELSE, which currently costs $43.94. Any suggestions?

Many Owe Health to Cancer Victim

Article #71
The News Courier, June 13, 2010

Some of you who read this column may owe your health or life to a poor black lady who died in 1951 at thirty-one in Baltimore County, Md. This young mother of five died of ovarian cancer and had the human papillomavirus and syphilis. She died in the "colored" charity section of Johns Hopkins Hospital. Even though this lady died in 1951, she has traveled in space. Let me explain.

Mrs. Henrietta Lacks was a good mother and wife. Alive, she fed and gave comfort to those less fortunate. Dead, she has prevented people from having polio, helped people with cancer, and aided those with Parkinson's disease.

In January 1951, Lacks began experiencing bloody vaginal discharge and pain in her cervix. She went to Johns Hopkins on the first day of February and was diagnosed with cervical cancer. The examining physician had never seen a tumor like Henrietta's. Without her knowledge, cells from her carcinoma were removed for research purposes.

These cells were given to George Gey, the head of cancer research at the hospital; he noticed that Lacks's cells did something unusual. Lacks's cells lived, whereas others' cells that Gey had tested did not. They could be kept alive, and they could grow.

No one knows why. The human papillomavirus and syphilis would have weakened Lacks's immune system. Were these diseases contributory factors? No one knows.

Three years after Lacks's death, Dr. Jonas Salk used her cells to create the polio vaccine. A factory at Tuskegee Institute in Alabama was created to mass-produce her cells, known as HeLa cells (Lacks's initials). The factory produced almost three trillion of her cells a week, sending them to the far corners of the world for medical research.

It is estimated that approximately fifty million metric tons of her cells have been produced.

They have been used to study AIDS, gene mapping, the effects of radiation and toxic substances on human cells, and many other scientific endeavors. Also, Lacks's cells have gone into space and were the first cells to be cloned.

So how did her five children and husband feel about Lacks's cells helping millions of people? They did not even know. They were not told anything until twenty-five years after she died.

Since the family learned of their mother's benevolence, have they benefited financially? Not a bit. The family has received nothing from what was and is a goldmine for medical and scientific research. A small vial of HeLa cells sells for $250. Remember that fifty million metric tons of her cells have been produced. Her family lives in poverty and cannot afford health care or the drugs her cells have made possible.

Some readers may be fortunate because you owe your health to this unfortunate woman. Sometimes those we know the least help us the most, and those we know the most help us the least.

Sources: The Immortal Life of Henrietta Lacks by Rebecca Skloot; USA TODAY, March 9, 2010; and various websites.

Does Reading This Column Use Your Entire Brain?

Article #72
The News Courier, September 5, 2010

Pychomythology is that shady area of my discipline that many believe but is not true.

The myths are numerous and have been soundly disproven by solid scientific research. Sadly, they hang around to mislead and deceive people. People spend good money on bad self-help gurus who convince the unknowing what they need to know.

I may write about several of these in the coming months if time permits. Today I discuss one of the most pervasive myths: humans use only 10 percent of their brains.

People, we use 100 percent of our brains and always have.

It is uncertain when and where this myth started. Some argue it may have originated with William James and his 1890 publication, *The Principles of Psychology*.

He doubted the average human achieved more than 10 percent of their intellectual potential. "Intellectual potential" and "brain" are not the same. Moreover, and more importantly, James's statement 120 years ago was based on conjecture and assumption, not scientific research. Furthermore, in the best-selling 1936 book by Dale Carnegie, *How to Win Friends and Influence People*, Lowell Thomas claimed in the preface that William James said humans use only 10 percent of their brains.

Another explanation for the 10 percent belief is that for every nerve cell in the brain, there are approximately nine to ten glial cells.

Neuroglial (nerve glue) serves important functions in the brain, such as keeping it clean and creating insulation for the nerve cells. Glial cells are active, alert, and ambitious in making the brain work efficiently.

Glial cells are much smaller than nerve cells, even though they outnumber nerve cells ten to one; the brain, volume-wise, is 50 percent neurons and 50 percent glial. Regardless of how the myth started, it is still widely believed today.

How do we know we use 100 percent of our brain? Scientific research on healthy and unhealthy brains tells us.

Direct scientific research on the healthy brain is accomplished through various sophisticated brain imaging technologies. For instance, medicine has functional magnetic resonance imaging (MRI), positron emission tomography (PET) scanners, electroencephalograms (EEGs), and others. Trust me; such procedures reveal, without question, that the entire brain is used as we go about our daily life.

As for indirect evidence, think about it. When a human has a stroke or suffers other brain trauma that affects only a small portion of the brain, say 5 percent, it can lead to significant behavioral and cognitive deficits. If we had a 90 percent reserve in the brain, a 5 percent reduction should not cause significant impairment.

Finally, evolution speaks against retaining something we do not use. Body parts that evolved over millenniums were used and thus useful. The 10 percent use of the brain belongs to the shady area known as Pycho-mythology; the 100 percent use of the brain belongs to psychological and physiological reality. Let us walk in the light, not the shade.

Misconception Matters with Infantile Autism

Article #73
The News Courier, September 29, 2010

Has there recently been an epidemic of infantile autism? Are infant vaccinations, those containing the preservative thimerosal, the culprit? The answer is probably "no" for both questions.

I know this is an answer many people, especially parents of autistic children, do not want to hear and do not believe. But it must be written. Misconceptions matter and can even be deadly. Needless outbreaks of measles are occurring in countries such as Austria, Italy, Switzerland, England, and even areas in the United States where parents fear vaccinations can cause infantile autism.

This argument is one of those issues that has become intense because of the changes in the definition of the term being discussed. Definitions can change over time due to people using a word differently, or a definition can change when people in authority alter the definition. The so-called epidemic of infantile autism is due to the latter.

The Diagnostic and Statistical Manual of Mental Disorders is the "bible" used by psychiatrists and psychologists to classify mental disorders. It has gone through several revisions, illustrating that the classification of mental disorders is not an exact science.

In the very first DSM, published in 1952, autism did not exist as a separate category; Thus, there was not a distinct autistic diagnosis, and no one was considered autistic. In the DSM II, released in 1968, there still was not an autistic category. It was not until 1980 that the manual's third edition included diagnostic information about "infantile autism."

In 1987, the DSM-III Revised edition was published. In this edition, the six criteria were expanded to sixteen, and a person only had to have eight of them to be classified as autistic. Based on a combination formula from statistics, there were now approximately 10,000 combinations allowing a person to be classified as autistic.

In 1994, another revision of the DSM was published, the DSM IV. In this edition, more subtypes were added to the autistic category. So, what do these changes have to do with the definition of autism by those in authority in 1987 and 1994?

Simply, there should have been a very large increase in the number of people diagnosed with this condition. After 1994 and until 2003, the number of diagnoses jumped tremendously.

There has not been an epidemic of autism, and vaccinations do not put children at risk for it. However, not vaccinating a child for things like measles can be deadly.

Educators Fall Prey to the Power of Ignorance

Article #74
The News Courier, December 5, 2010

There are four types of ignorance. Trust me; I have been ignorant in all four of them. Some types are more ignorant than others. There is ignorance, and then there is real ignorance.

The first type is called "lack of knowledge." This is the least ignorant of the types and may be the beginning of wisdom. This is when you know that you do not know. For instance, I know that I do not know calculus. I have never studied it. "Lack of knowledge" ignorance does not mean that you are too dumb to learn; it means you do not know it now. It means you are aware of your ignorance about the issue being discussed. You know that you do not know.

But what if you are unaware of your ignorance? This type of ignorance is named "lack of awareness." In other words, you do not know that you do not know. Have you ever been around people who talk as if they know about everything but are clueless about many things? At sixty, I realized I did not know jack about many things I talked about in my twenties and thirties. These people, like me, never heeded Abraham Lincoln's advice. Lincoln said, "It's better to remain quiet and be thought to be a fool than to open your mouth and remove all doubt." Many times, I removed all doubt.

The third type of ignorance is unsettling and can be dangerous. It is known as a "lack of acceptance." Have you known people who will argue with a signpost? Such people do not accept what has been proven to be true. Believe it or not, some still claim the earth is flat and the sun revolves around Earth. When I was young, I was taught not to believe in evolution and did not for many years. I do now because the evidence is all around us and is too overwhelming not to believe.

The fourth and final type of ignorance is lack of critical thinking." This is when people believe something that has never been shown to be true when placed under scientific investigation. Examples are people who believe in ESP, channeling, astral projection, and psychic ability. Again, when I was younger, I tended to believe in some paranormal claims. It may be fun to believe in such things, but it is not realistic.

152 | EDUCATORS FALL PREY TO THE POWER OF IGNORANCE

Some argue that psychic ability (or other examples) has never been disproved. No one can prove a negative. If someone claims something extraordinary, that someone must prove it.

As I write, a psychic has never done anything a magician cannot do. James Randi, a world-famous magician, has a $1 million standing offer to any psychic who can perform a feat that Randi cannot. This offer has existed for many years, and no psychic is a million dollars richer.

Is it not the mission of education to remove ignorance? Ignorance can be deadly. Recognizing the different types is the first step toward a safer and saner world. But sadly, many educators fall prey to the mind-numbing power of ignorance. Me included.

Most Resolutions Center Around the Human Emotion of Happiness

Article #75
The News Courier, January 2, 2011

At this time of year, many people make New Year's resolutions. That is commendable. Setting goals is good for mental health; if we reach them during the year, the dividends are even more pleasant.

But let us reflect for a moment. Do not most New Year resolutions center around one human emotion: happiness? I will be happier if I lose weight; I will be happier if I do not spend too much money; I will be happier if I find that certain someone; and the list goes on and on because, ultimately, we all want to be happier with ourselves.

So, on the advent of this New Year, please let an old psychology professor relate what research has revealed about happiness.

- To the surprise of many, happiness has a very strong genetic component. If you received a healthy dose of the "happy gene," you are fortunate. If not, your happiness will take more work. Martha Washington, the wife of our first president, once said, "The greater part of our happiness or misery depends on our dispositions, not our circumstances." My father, Darwin Durm, told me many times when I was a young boy, "Happiness is a state of mind." For some, achieving that state of mind is genetically easier than for others.
- The genetic influence creates in each individual his own happiness "set point." Regardless of what happens to us in our external environment, each of us will bounce up if it is a good circumstance and down if it is a bad situation. But, we will eventually return to our previous genetic set point. For example, research has shown that big lottery winners will bounce way up for about two months and return to their previous happiness.
- Conversely, people who have been paralyzed from the waist down (paraplegics) due to an accident will bounce down in happiness. After a few months, however, most will return closely (albeit not completely) to their previous set point.

- It seems there may be some monumental events in people's lives that, for some, may be very difficult to bounce back from in the short term. For example, some are being divorced, widowed, and losing a child. For many, but not all, they will eventually adapt in the long run.
- Can money buy happiness? It seems $50,000 may make it cheaper! Research reveals that if a family's total income is less than this amount, their happiness goes down. Being unable to pay the bills and provide the necessities is inversely related to happiness. However, when the income is above $50,000, the connection between money and happiness disappears.
- Even though genetics (aptitude) plays a role in happiness, attitude is also important in this happiness game. You have heard the adage about the half glass of milk—either half empty or half full. For those with a good dose of the happy gene, it will more naturally be half full. But if you are determined, you can pour more milk into the glass.

In conclusion, as you create your New Year resolutions, which tend to center around happiness, please remember that you may not have had any "say-so" about the glass container. However, you can search and find more milk. May you have a Happy New Year!

ASSIST Serves as Athens State's 'Marine Corps'

Article #76
The News Courier, March 6, 2011

We who are older sometimes belittle the activities of the younger.

We who are older sometimes believe that those younger are not as caring and helpful as they should be. Not so for our marine corps at Athens State University. Yes, I know, there are no marine corps at Athens State. But we do have a group nicknamed ASSIST for Athens State University. Involved in Social Togetherness, they are the few, the proud, and the strong.

This ASSIST group is the Student United Way Club on campus. They are the first and only Student United Way Club on a college campus in Alabama. I am extremely proud of them. Let me explain why.

The club formed this past fall at the encouragement of Kaye McFarlen, the Director of the Athens-Limestone United Way. There are two co-presidents, Carissa Behel and Erin Minor. They serve, by virtue of their office, on the board of the local United Way. Active members are in alphabetical order, Tanya Campbell, Tami King, April Laycock, who serves as secretary, Alicia Longmore-Marston, and Tami Schoenberger.

These young ladies fed many people over the Thanksgiving and Christmas holidays. How? They collected over 1,000 cans of food they donated to the food pantry of the Limestone County Churches Involved.

In the fall, they raked leaves and "winterized" a house for an elderly lady in Athens in cooperation with CASA. Before Christmas, they decorated a truck and marched in the Athens Christmas Parade, the only Athens State club to do so. Also, for the holidays, they drove to Huntsville. They packed hundreds of bags for the "Toys for Tots" program for Limestone County families.

They just finished painting the exterior of an entire house in conjunction with the Athens-Limestone County Habitat for Humanity.

They are currently planning to organize classes later this spring on how to collect and use food coupons to stretch the food budget for needy families. They hope to provide childcare for this event so more mothers can attend.

These marine corps women are trying to organize a talent contest for students and faculty later this semester to increase student activities on campus and recruit more members for the club to do more for the community.

As a college professor for thirty-four years, I can attest to the fact that certain groups of students stand out more than others. There are years when I remember groups of students that just seem to do more, learn more, socialize better, and are simply a joy to teach. I have years where I do not have those memories.

The former group of students I will remember for the rest of my life. I will remember them for their determination in the classroom but especially for their dedication to the larger classroom and the world outside those academic walls. They have fed the hungry, kept the older warmer during winter, and they have worked to ensure children would smile on Christmas morning. They are Athens State's marine corps; they are the few, the proud, the strong.

Could Jesus Have Been Forty-three When He Died?

Article #77
The News Courier, April 24, 2011

"You are not yet fifty years old," the Jews said to him [Jesus], "and you have seen Abraham!" (John 8:57).

Since this is Easter, I will offer the thesis that Jesus was in his midforties when he was crucified, not thirty-one or thirty-three, as widely believed. I will offer those arguments that are historical and those that come from the Bible.

The Bible says, "now Jesus himself was about thirty years old when he began his ministry" (Luke 3:23). However, nowhere in the Bible does it say Jesus was in his early thirties when he died. The belief arose in relation to how often Jesus visited Jerusalem in his ministry, once in the Gospel of Mark and three times in the Gospel of John. In Jesus's day, all devout Jews in his part of the world visited Jerusalem at the time of Passover.

Therefore, if he was "about thirty" and visited Jerusalem only once, it is argued he was thirty-one at his death, or if he visited three times, he was thirty-three. But these are only the times recorded in the Bible when Jesus visited Jerusalem. Let us remember what is written in the last verse of the Gospel of John, "Jesus did many other things as well. If every one of them were written down, I suppose that even the world would not have room for the books that would be written." (John 21:25)

Let us also be aware that the passage of time is unchangeable but that the recording of that passage of time is very changeable. This is where Dennis the Short (Dionysius Exiguous to his peers) enters the narrative. Each one of us is influenced every day of our lives by Dennis. Dennis is the one that changed the way we keep time.

This year is AD 2011 (AD means "in the year of our Lord" and not "After Death"). Anno Domini time is based on Jesus's birth. But understand there was never an AD 111 or AD 211 or AD 311 or AD 411, or AD 511. It was not until approximately 500 years after Jesus died did his birth become the starting point for counting time.

Due to this column's brevity, it is sufficient to write that Dennis the Short was a sixth-century Scythian monk, an amateur astronomer, and a translator of ecclesiastical canons. Dennis did not like Anno Diocletian time (based on the Roman emperor Diocletian). Thus he changed the year 248 Anno Diocletian to 532 Anno Domini. He counted backward but was off by four to seven years. Devout biblical scholars and even my NIV Bible's timeline place Jesus's birth at 6 BC to 5 BC (using Anno Domini time). The time of his birth is verifiable from different sources. Therefore Jesus must have been born around 6 or 5 BC at the latest. Primarily 6 or 5 BC is credible because of Herod the king's death in 4 BC. Therefore, according to Matthew 2:16, Jesus must have been at least two years old when this Herod died. Herod's death is easily documented.

Now let us look at the time of Jesus's death. According to the Bible, Jesus died after John the Baptist. Therefore, the date of John the Baptist's death is very important to this argument. John the Baptist's date of death, ranges from AD 23 up to AD 36, according to different sources. More and more present-day scholars believe that the AD 36 date is more correct.

Moreover, the writing of Josephus, the Jewish historian, who lived during this time and wrote about John, supports the AD 36 date. If Jesus died after John, then say Jesus died in AD 37. If I start with 6 BC for Jesus's birth and add up to AD 37, I have Jesus as at least forty-three years old, if not older, at his crucifixion.

There is another strong argument that Jesus was in his midforties when he died. Irenaeus, the Bishop of Lyon, an early Christian writer who lived approximately between AD 125-191, wrote in his principal work *Against Heresies* that apostolic oral tradition related that Jesus was almost fifty when he died. Again, this is an oral tradition based on the original apostles of Jesus.

Therefore, if Jesus was in his midforties or older, his ministry lasted thirteen to eighteen years. Thus, the Jews said to Jesus in John 8:57, "You are not yet fifty years old."

The Stubbornness of Misinformation
Part 1 of 2

Article #78
The News Courier, July 3, 2011

If presented with facts, it makes sense that we should adjust our thinking to accommodate those facts. We should. Research suggests that many of us do not.

In an earlier column, I wrote about three kinds of ignorance. The first (possibly the beginning of wisdom) is when you know you do not know. Second, you do not know that you do not know (naive and dangerous because you can be easily deceived). Third, you do not accept what is known.

The third form of ignorance is my focus in this column. It may be the most detrimental. As a teacher of critical thinking at the university level, I thought few people, the most stubborn, fell into this category. I was wrong. Most people fall into this category if the issue is one they hold dear, such as politics, gun control, or healthcare.

As we prepare to celebrate our country's democracy this July Fourth, Joe Keohane has written an article that we need to heed. His article is entitled "Researchers Discover a Surprising Threat to Democracy: Our Brains." He explains that a series of studies at the University of Michigan revealed that when most misinformed people are shown correct information, they do not change their minds. Indeed, their belief in incorrect information becomes stronger.

Scholar James Kuklinski's research revealed that misinformed people often have the strongest political opinions. The more misinformed one is the stronger one's opinion. Studies have shown similar patterns on topics such as education, healthcare reform, immigration, and gun control. Can the same be said for religion?

Such stubbornness is influenced by "selective perception" and "selective recall." Both operate against sound, rational thinking. Selective perception occurs when one recognizes what reinforces existing beliefs. If I believe the full moon causes strange behavior, and I notice a full moon on a "crazy night," my belief in the correlation is reinforced. On crazy nights with no full moon, I do not note the absence of the correlative factor.

Selective recall means I believe in the correlation because I remember crazy nights when the moon was full and forget those that occurred without a full moon.

In other words, I notice what supports what I already believe and remember only those events that support my belief.

A third factor contributing to erroneous thinking is people's tendency to watch tv channels or read books, blogs, or magazines that reinforce what they already believe. Conservatives watch FOX, and liberals watch MSNBC. Neither learns much that they do not already know or believe.

His thoughts on misinformation will be continued on next week's Opinion page.

The Stubbornness of Misinformation
Part 2 of 2

Article #79
The News Courier, July 10, 2011

Last week I addressed how stubborn we can be even when shown we are wrong. Indeed, even when offered correct information, we tend to persist in believing what is incorrect. I shared three factors that contribute to our misinformed stubbornness.

Today, I address the relationship between children's self-esteem and stubbornness about misinformation. Although many of my fellow psychologists would disagree, I think it is wrong to teach children that they are always right. Think about it. If a child is never told he is wrong, why would he entertain that he might be when he is grown, even when offered evidence?

In his popular book, *The Six Pillars of Self-Esteem*, Nathaniel Branden claimed that one "cannot think of a single psychological problem—from anxiety and depression to fear of intimacy or success to spouse battery or child molestation—that is not traceable to the problem of low self-esteem." I strongly disagree with Branden.

Teachers will tell you that many discipline problems occur among children with high self-esteem that may have been built on false foundations.

Think about it. Of what value is a trophy if all who play get one? How valuable is an A in an academic course if all students get As? Winning trophies means more to those who have lost out on them previously. Likewise, an A is noteworthy if only a few students get one.

According to an article by S. Salerno, some schools refer to children who are poor spellers as "individual spellers" for fear of hurting children's feelings. In my opinion, one can be as "individual" as one wants, but many vocations require the ability to spell.

In college classes, students have asked, "Do you take off points for spelling?" I answer, "Yes." I have often been asked in my statistics class, "Do you take off points if I work the problem right but get the wrong answer?"

I answer, "If you had worked the problem right, you would have gotten the right answer." Many students think I am difficult. Life can be difficult.

Readers who think I am wrong about self-esteem ought to review a comprehensive analysis of over 15,000 studies that investigated self-esteem to every imaginable psychological variable. The meta-analysis was done by Roy Baumeister, Jennifer Campbell, Joachim Krueger, and Kathleen Vohs and published in 2008 in the *Psychological Science in the Public Interest* journal. Their findings went against common opinion. That is, they found that self-esteem is minimally related to personal success.

In conclusion, let me return to my original thesis. Stubbornness is positive if one tries to overcome obstacles and strengthen weaknesses when navigating everyday life. Stubbornness is negative when one holds onto an opinion that can be proven wrong.

Sources: 50 Great Myths of Popular Psychology by Scott Lilienfeld et al., lecture notes, and others.

Alabama's Family Values: A Second Look

Article #80
The News Courier, January 21, 2012

A few years ago, I wrote an article entitled *"A Closer Look at Alabama's Family Values."* I received many comments about it. Today, I take a second look. Remember that I offer this piece as food for critical thought, not criticism.

Family values should concern the entire family and the treatment of each individual in that family from birth to death. Therefore, let us start with infancy. Who has more value than an infant? Over 36 percent of children in Alabama are born out of wedlock (the national average is 35.7 percent), and one child in ten is born with low birth weight, ranking Alabama third in that category. Moreover, Alabama is sixth in the nation in infant mortality rate. We rank very low in the care we give our youngest citizens, starting with nutrition when they are fetuses.

As Alabama children age, the care we give them ranks among the lowest in the nation.

We are seventh in the nation in the percentage of households headed by a single parent. What values are we passing on to our young people?

As Alabama children reach their teen years, life doesn't get much better, especially for young ladies. Our state ranks ninth in the nation regarding the teenage birth rate. What happened to the values of which we are so proud?

As Alabamian children reach adulthood, they find themselves in a state with a divorce rate that ranks fourth in the nation, a poverty level that ranks seventh, and ninth in receipt of public aid and food stamps.

Furthermore, we cannot praise our success when paying personal debt. Alabama ranks fourth in the nation in the personal bankruptcy rate.

In Alabama, senior citizens' treatment is not admirable. We rank tenth in the nation for the number of senior citizens living in poverty and third for the age-adjusted death rate. (Age-adjusted rates eliminate the distorting effects of the aging of the population.)

In my opinion, people holding governmental positions in Alabama and our church leadership should seek ways to improve our family values.

They should address ways to improve infant care, lift children out of poverty, and reduce teen pregnancy. We should search for new ways to improve the life of the Alabama adult, help the family stay intact, and make us more accountable financially.

Paraphrasing the novelist Ayn Rand, we may ignore reality, but we can never ignore the consequences of reality. Let's not ignore our real values and work together to improve them.

(This information was taken from "State Rankings" 17th edition, edited by Kathleen and Scott Morgan, and published by Morgan Quitno Press.)

Misleading Statistics Lead to Mistaken Thinking

Article #81
The News Courier, February 19, 2012

I have coined a new term—"Mistakestistics." The term refers to thinking gone awry due to misleading statistics. Marriage, divorce, and cuckoldry as examples of Mistakestistics.

We are led to believe certain things about marriage and divorce that are untrue. Some deceptions are easier to see than others. It is hardest to spot deceptions that use numbers. When information is given in numbers or "quantified," it seems more credible. For instance, the divorce rate in America is calculated based on the per capita annual marriage rate per 1,000 people compared to the annual divorce rate per 1,000 people. The divorce rate in America is 50 percent. However, 50 percent of all marriages in America do not end in divorce.

Let me explain. For argument's sake, let us say there will be 100 marriages in Limestone County in 2012 and fifty divorces. Most couples who divorced this year were not married in 2012. People who divorce tend to divorce more than once. Thus, many of the fifty couples who divorce this year in Limestone County will have divorced before. Therefore, a few people account for more divorces. Thus, the success rate of marriages is really above 50 percent.

We are led to believe that if a marriage lasts more than seven years, its success rate increases. Why? The average length of a marriage before a divorce is seven years. Few divorces occur at seven years. How can this be?

Seven years is the "arithmetic average," a.k.a. the "mean," of the length of a marriage before a divorce. There are two modes when it comes to divorce—most divorce occurs after three years of marriage or after twenty-two years of marriage. Divorce is a bi-modal distribution. A "mode" in a distribution is the "score" with the highest frequency.

Couples who divorce after three years tend to love and lust after each other but may not like each other. Once the lust wears off, the marriage deteriorates.

Couples who divorce after twenty-two years often wait until the children are grown and gone. These couples may like each other but no longer love each other. Of the two modes of divorce, after three years of marriage is the most common.

A third misleading statistic about marriage and family relates to "cuckoldry." Cuckoldry occurs when a man who thinks he is the father of a child isn't the real biological father. He is a cuckold; he has been duped. Apparently, cuckoldry tends to be highest for first and last-born children in a family.

Some studies suggest that the cuckoldry rate is 10 to 15 percent. Others claim it is as high as 20 to 30 percent. Studies also claim the cuckoldry rate is higher in large cities where it is easier to protect anonymity compared to rural settings where everyone knows your business.

But back to the 10 to 15 percent figures. It is worth questioning the figures. The more accurate scientific studies put the rate at less than 4 percent.

There is merit in questioning and studying reports with numbers. Just because an argument uses numbers doesn't mean it is correct. Be careful not to form mistaken thoughts based on misleading statistics—"Mistakestistics."

Patriotism and the Type of War

Article #82
The News Courier, April 8, 2012

Patriotism is a good thing. It is good to be loyal to your country. In my opinion, citizens' patriotism depends on several interacting factors. The strength of these factors ebbs and flows depending on the kind of war underway.

If a country attacks your homeland, patriotism surges. Three additional variables influence the intensity of patriotism: the length and cost of the war and the amount of your blood involved in the conflict.

There is an inverse relationship between the cost of a war and the intensity of patriotism. The same is true of the length of a war and patriotism. Conversely, the shorter the war, the greater the patriotism. America was very patriotic during Desert Storm. Even though America was not directly attacked, the war was short. I remember when the Mobile Army Surgical Hospital unit of which I was a member was treated to a hero's welcome when our plane landed in Dover, Delaware. No one in the MASH unit was a hero; we just did our duty.

The extent to which one's relatives are involved in a war influences the intensity of an individual's patriotism. It is easier to be patriotic if you don't have anyone involved in the war, even when it is long and costly and your country has not been attacked.

What constitutes the amount of blood in a war? The existence of a draft is the defining factor. If there is no draft and your sons, daughters, husbands, or wives do not have to fight, you pray for other people. But if you were like my paternal grandparents, who had three sons in World War II simultaneously, you get down on your knees and pray hard for your sons to return safely.

Let me pose a hypothetical question. If you were a parent with three children involved in a deadly war, would you rather win and lose your three children or lose the war and have all your children live? Tough question, but if a parent would rather their three children live, would you question their patriotism?

If a war lasted many years, was quite costly, our country was not attacked, and most who served were drafted, would patriotism be high? No. Think about Vietnam. If a war lasted many years, was very costly, and most who served were volunteers would patriotism be high? Yes. Think of Afghanistan. The degree of patriotism related to the war in Afghanistan is on the decline because of the cost and duration of the war. Still, there are no marches against the war and no burning of draft cards because there are no draft cards.

Yes, patriotism is a good thing. It is good to be loyal to your country. However, we should not ask the same young men and women to keep fighting in repeated deployments after so many years.

Your Worldview, Stretching, and Rubber Bands

Article #83
The News Courier, May 20, 2012

Today I want to talk about rubber bands, landing on the moon, an American desert, a person's worldview, my maternal grandmother, my paternal grandfather, a Swiss psychologist, and why the American government is at a standstill. Let us begin.

I was nineteen on July 20, 1969, when my paternal grandfather, Albert Durm, family members, and I watched his grainy black and white television as American astronauts landed on the moon. Pa traveled from Tennessee to Texas in a covered wagon when he was five. I turned to him and said, "Pa, we have come a long way in your lifetime." He smiled. "Yes, we have."

My maternal grandmother, Addie Hatchett, whom I loved very much, did not have a television and never believed we had landed on the moon. She thought the American government created the moon-landing scene somewhere in an American desert.

Pa Durm's and Granny Hatchett's worldviews were different. Pa could adapt by accommodating our landing on the moon. Granny Hatchett adapted by assimilating and refusing to believe it happened. That brings me to the Swiss psychologist Jean Piaget, born in 1896, the same year as my Pa Durm and nine years before my Granny Hatchett.

Piaget developed a cognitive (thinking) developmental theory that is still accepted and widely believed today. Piaget claimed that to develop normally, people must interact effectively with their environments from childhood to adulthood. He referred to effective interaction as "adaptation." Adaptation requires thinking skills and consists of two other concepts: "assimilation" and "accommodation."

When the environment presents new information to think about—such as a moon landing, for instance—one might reconsider their worldview or how one understands the world. When a person accommodates, he changes his thinking to incorporate new information; when a person assimilates, they change the information to align with their existing worldview.

Granny Hatchett could not accept astronauts landing on the moon. According to her worldview, as she said, "If God had wanted us on the moon, He would have put us there. He didn't, so we can't get there!" Therefore, Granny Hatchett made the new information fit what she already believed. She assimilated. In contrast, Pa Durm changed his worldview to accommodate the new information.

As a teacher, one hopes to create a learning environment where students accommodate new information by changing their worldviews according to what they learn. Good teaching is like stretching mental rubber bands. Once a rubber band is stretched, it can never return to its original size. If we are exposed only to what aligns with what we already know or believe, we will not learn anything. We must be willing to accommodate new information.

The legislative bodies of our governments, state and federal, are at a standstill because neither party, Republican nor Democrat, will accommodate; they only assimilate. Neither side will change its perspective to adjust to new information. Instead, they change the information to fit what they already believe. People who will not accommodate cognitively cannot accommodate politically.

As I said, rubber bands, landing on the moon, the desert, worldviews, my grandparents, a Swiss psychologist, and "frozen" legislative bodies are all connected.

Is America Becoming a Matriarchal Society?

Article #84
The News Courier, August 5, 2012

Is America becoming a matriarchal (female-dominated) society?

All young men who read this, take heed—be nice to women. If you live long enough, you will probably be working for one. There are several reasons to think America may become a matriarchal society. The reasons can be found in social, biological, financial, and educational realms, to name a few.

Today, I address the educational aspect.

What does education have to do with the trend toward a matriarchal society? In a nutshell, more women than men are going to college.

In my classes this summer at Athens State University, I have fifty-one females and thirteen males, or a ratio of 80:20. For many years, more women than men have attended Athens State University.

The trend has been occurring since 1991 throughout the entire United States. By 2005, women comprised 54 percent of college enrollment. By 2013, it is predicted that women will make up nearly 60 percent.

Nationwide, young men from low-income and middle-income families need to attend higher education but are underrepresented on college campuses. The South has the biggest gender gap, with a 140:100 female/male ratio.

Tamar Lewin wrote an article in the *New York Times* entitled "At Colleges, Women Are Leaving Men in the Dust." Lewin related that men are not only trailing women in enrollment but also study less, make lower grades, and fewer will graduate.

Furthermore, whether the institution is a community college, a small liberal arts institution, a public university, or an elite institution like Harvard, women receive more than their proportionate share of graduation honors.

Not only are women receiving a disproportionate share of baccalaureate graduation honors, but more women than men are going to graduate school.

In an article entitled "Men Grossly Underrepresented in Graduate School Enrollment," Mark J. Perry relates that in 2009 for the first time, more women than men attained doctorate degrees in all disciplines combined. There are still specific disciplines where more men get doctorates, such as business, engineering, health sciences, mathematics, and computer science.

Women, however, earn more doctorates in public administration, social and behavioral sciences, education, arts and humanities, and even biological and agricultural sciences.

Thus far, I have used data to illustrate my point. Now I offer proof based on personal observation. I usually scan the "engaged to be married" sections in the local newspapers, looking for current or former students. Usually, the announcement lists the educational backgrounds and employers of each person. Over the past several years, I have noticed that brides-to-be have more education than prospective grooms. Also, brides-to-be tend to be employed in professional fields. One may assume they will provide medical, dental, and other benefits for the family.

"Providing for the family" seems to fall more frequently on women in our society. Therefore, if this trend continues, we will slowly become a matriarchal society.

Race, Color, Creed: Is There Such a Thing as 'Equality?'

Article #85
The News Courier, September 23, 2012

Over the past several weeks in the local community, much has been written about "unfairness" and "prejudice." Here, I offer my two cents worth on these issues.

To begin, I ask two questions. Have we not become a society in which we turned the concept of equal treatment "*regardless* of race, color, or creed" into a doctrine of "*regardful*" of race, color, or creed?" If so, what happens to justice? As Alexander Hamilton, a founding father of our country, once noted, "the first duty of society is justice."

Justice and fairness revolve around two issues—ability and treatment. Below is a 2-by-2 matrix I designed and used in my classes to discuss these concepts at Athens State University.

		ABILITY	
		Equal	Unequal
TREATMENT	Equal	A Best World	B Unfair
	Unequal	C Prejudice	D Worst World

Condition A is the best of worlds.

People receive equal treatment for equal ability in an ideal world for which we should strive. If people with equal abilities are treated the same, then all have been treated justly. To paraphrase Hamilton, society has done its first duty.

In Condition B, we have an unfair world where people are treated equally and do not have the same abilities. If a person has more ability than someone else and both receive the same pay, resentment surfaces. If any high school, college, or professional coach was told all players must play the same amount of time regardless of ability, they would laugh. Yet, some employers are told that all employees must be treated equally.

All employees should be treated equally—to a point. The more able, harder-working individual should be rewarded. If they are not, it is an unfair world.

Condition C is where prejudice enters the picture. Two people with equal abilities receive different treatment. One is prejudged, incorrectly, to be less able than the other. If one claims prejudice, he must show he has an equal ability. If he cannot, has prejudice occurred? Many people claim discrimination; few people can prove it.

Finally, we come to Condition D, the worst world of all—unequal treatment for unequal ability. Some people receive better treatment and have less ability. Alternatively, people with more ability get treated worse. Let the fireworks begin.

When I was at Ole Miss working on my doctorate, my classmates chided me because I referred to my professors as "doctor." Many of them called their professors by their first names. I did not because I was not their equal. Elsewhere, I was a captain in the military, sitting in the barracks with three other captains when a major entered.

We called him "major." He said we should call him by his first name since we were off duty. We didn't, however, because we were not his equal.

My son, Spencer, is on the seventh-grade football team at Athens Middle School. He is not on the first team because his ability is not first-team level.

I am, however, very proud of him. He enjoys the game, and I encourage him to keep hustling and working.

I have explained to my son what I call the Abraham Lincoln philosophy. In his early life, Lincoln wrote, "I will prepare myself, and if the opportunity ever comes, I will be ready."

He did, it did, and he was. I tell Spencer to keep preparing.

Notice that Lincoln wrote, "if the opportunity ever comes...." America has tried to ensure "equal opportunity" for all citizens as it should. But equal opportunity does *not* mean equal results. Do not cry "prejudice" if you have not prepared yourself. Work harder if you live in an unfair world where you have more ability but are treated the same as those with less ability. Hopefully, your opportunity will come, and society will have done its first duty.

If we could live in the Best World (Condition "A"), everyone with equal ability would be treated equally *regardless* of race, color, or creed. No one would receive special treatment because (*regardful*) of race, color, or creed.

There, that is my two cents worth.

Guns Not the Cause of Sandy Hook Shootings

Article #86
The News Courier, January 6, 2013

For many years I have heard, "guns do not kill people; people kill people."

That is true, but guns contribute to killing people. In other words, one cannot say that guns cause death, just as one cannot say that cigarettes cause lung cancer. Let me explain.

I tell my Critical Thinking class that I could write the causes of events that are known for certain on one page. It would probably not take a whole page. It is incorrect to say that the polio virus causes polio. In 2013, we know so few true causes, despite the advanced technology at our disposal.

To establish true causality, one must show that a condition, such as a gun, is necessary and sufficient for an effect (e.g., killing a person) to occur. Many people have been killed without a gun; thus, a gun is unnecessary. A necessary condition is a condition that must exist for an effect to occur.

A sufficient condition is a condition that will always produce the effect. The presence of a gun does not always produce the killing of a person. Therefore, guns do not cause the death of a person; they are neither necessary nor sufficient.

Likewise, cigarette smoking technically does not cause lung cancer. Many people have died of lung cancer and never smoked a single cigarette. Thus, cigarette smoking is not necessary for lung cancer. Moreover, many people have smoked heavily and not developed lung cancer. Therefore, cigarette smoking is not sufficient to cause lung cancer.

I mentioned that the polio virus does not cause polio. Here is why. No one has ever had polio that did not first have the polio virus. Thus, the virus is "necessary" for polio.

However, some people have the polio virus but not the disease. Although the virus is necessary, it is not sufficient to cause the crippling disease. What else is required? We do not know. As you can see, one sheet of paper can contain the most known true causes.

Let us say you are driving your car. Unbeknownst to you, your fan belt breaks, and you keep driving. Your car engine will overheat. Your broken fan belt was sufficient to produce the heated engine. Other events can produce an overheated engine, such as a hole in your radiator; therefore, the broken fan belt does not have to exist for an overheated engine to occur. It is sufficient but not necessary. It will always produce that effect if you keep driving, but it is unnecessary.

Let us return to my original premise; even though guns are neither necessary nor sufficient to kill a person, their presence contributes to killing a single person or many people. Let us use common sense—if the young man who recently killed the innocent people in Connecticut had not had access to an assault weapon in his fit of rage, some of those children might not have lost their lives.

It is unlikely that the same number of children would have died if he'd had only a knife. According to the British Broadcasting Corporation, on December 14, at about the same time as the Connecticut school tragedy occurred, Min Youngjun entered a school in the Chinese village of Chenpeng and injured twenty-three people. He did not kill a single person. He had only a knife.

The polio virus alone does not cause polio; it contributes to it. Cigarette smoking alone does not cause lung cancer; it contributes to it. Guns alone do not kill innocent people; their use contributes to deaths.

If we continue to deny this, society must accept the frequent killing of innocent people as normal.

Next week, I will consider what may have contributed to the Sandy Hook tragedy, including mental illness and violent video culture. I will also offer a comparative analysis of nations and guns.

Guns Contribute to Killing People

Article #87
The News Courier, January 13, 2013

Last week, I explained that it might be true that guns do not kill people, but they contribute to killing people.

This week, let us look at two other contributors to the very high homicide rate in the United States: the violent video culture of our society and mental illness. Before we discuss those, let us learn first how America compares to other countries in the number of firearms owned.

Sources differ, but America has about 4 to 5 percent of the world's population. It is estimated that we have between 40 and 50 percent of all guns worldwide. How does the number of firearms owned per citizen relate to the gun homicide rate of those countries? Let us use as our source a recent UN Office on Drugs and Crimes report, which compared 207 countries and territories.

The United States gun homicide rate per 100,000 people is thirty times that of France and Australia and thirty-three times higher than England and Wales. Overall, the United States gun homicide rate is twelve times higher than the average for other developed countries.

Does this mean the US is a tremendously more violent culture than the other countries in the world? Yes, and no. "Yes," for gun homicide and "No" for most other crimes such as theft, burglary, robbery, assaults, and others. Our rate for the latter crimes is within the range of other advanced countries.

Another important question concerns the relationship between violent behavior and violent video games. The answer is not as clear as one would think. One can find scientific studies that report a positive correlation; the more violent video games played, the more violent the behavior.

Then there are scientific studies that report a negative correlation—the more violent the video, the less violent the behavior. This finding gives credence to the "cathartic effect" belief; it is a mental kicking of the tire, allowing one to vent frustration without hurting anyone.

Thus, as you can see, it is not clear what the effect of violent video games is. I know this; if I may use the terminology I used in last week's column, watching violent video games is neither necessary nor sufficient for an individual to be violent. There was very violent behavior way before violent videos came on the scene.

A side note of interest here is Japan. Japan has a very high level, if not the highest, use of video games in the world, many of them very violent. Japan has strong gun control. Japan's gun homicide rate, however, is close to zero.

I believe the relationship between mental illness and crime is more important than a person playing violent video games and their connection to mass shootings.

The effect of mental illness on mass shootings, taken as a stand-alone contributor, has probably less impact than guns but more impact than violent video games. But what constitutes mental illness? Is there international agreement on that definition? Maybe for the more severe, but not for the less severe types. The individual states of America cannot agree on what is "mentally defective." One state passed a law not allowing a mentally defective person to own a gun. Good, but how is mentally defective defined by that particular state? The state does not give a definition. Therefore, law-enforcement agencies are back to square one.

Even psychologists and psychiatrists have difficulty reaching a consensus on diagnosing the diseased mind. In one important study, ten mental health professionals were individually shown the same video of a person who displayed mental problems. Each was instructed to give his diagnosis. Of the ten diagnoses, there were six different labels. Whew!

In conclusion, of the three contributing factors to mass homicide that we have addressed, the prevalence of guns, the playing of violent video games, and the presence of mental illness, it seems the number of firearms in a society is the strongest contributor to the crime. For instance, if one compares other nations to America and these other countries have similar rates of violent video use and levels of mental illness but fewer guns, they have a much lower gun homicide rate. One cannot compare the US to developed countries with more guns. None exist.

In the opening paragraph of last week's column, I wrote that guns do not kill people; people kill people. That is an exact answer to the wrong question: "Do guns kill people?" There is no need to ask, "do guns by themselves kill people?" John Tukey, the pioneering statistician, once wrote, "It is better to have an approximate answer to the right question than an exact answer to the wrong one."

Having fewer guns is the best approximate answer to the right question: "how do we best prevent innocent people from being killed?" It is more accurate than mental illness or violent video games.

'Commencement' is the Beginning, Not the End

Article #88
The News Courier, June 2, 2013

During May, commencement ceremonies were held in high schools, colleges, and universities across Alabama and the United States.

For many graduates, it was the conclusion of their formal education. Some will never go beyond high school, and others will never go beyond an undergraduate college degree.

But "commencement" means "beginning" and not "conclusion." Why is graduation called commencement? How can you graduate from something if you are only beginning?

Graduation is a rite of passage to adulthood. It signifies a transitional stage from an uneducated person to an educated one. The student begins the rest of their life having attained a certain level of learning. But no student should not stop learning.

Too many students stop learning once they graduate. They welcome the freedom from "book learning" and thinking. Yet, this is the opposite of what the degree means. Hopefully, the high school diploma or the college degree has prepared them to commence learning in the real world. They are now ready to read, learn, and think more. Sadly, many quit trying to learn.

The problems societies face are difficult to solve. The hardest problems people face are people problems.

Let me give you an example. If a man is driving his vehicle down the road and a flat tire occurs, the flat tire is easy to fix. If the motor of his car develops an oil leak, it might be fixed, albeit harder to repair. How do we fix the problem of the driver texting or calling on his telephone while driving?

We can warn smokers that smoking contributes to lung cancer, but many continue to smoke. We can warn that excessive drinking of alcohol can cause multiple problems, but many do not listen. We can warn that meth is very dangerous, but people continue to use it.

We can justifiably argue that if you have children, you should be responsible for them, but many are not. These are all people's problems. People's problems are not easy to solve. Solving people problems requires more book learning and more thinking, not less.

What I am about to write will offend some readers, but I must write it. Common sense will not solve many people's problems. If the solutions were so easy and common, the problems wouldn't continue to exist.

Most advances that have helped people have come as the result of book learning. For instance, it is not common sense that we give you a little of the disease to prevent you from having a disease. That is called vaccination.

Job applications request how many years of book sense (years of education) one has, not how many years of common sense. Those who belittle education the most have the least of it.

Graduates, you are commencing the rest of your life. Continue to read, learn, and think. The more you learn, the less you will think you know. There are no easy answers to society's greatest problems. We need your help.

Some Things in Life I Do Not Understand

Article #89
The News Courier

As a little boy, I hoed and "suckered" tobacco crops. As a teenager, after cutting the tobacco, I would hang it on the top rung in the barn, next to the tin roof. Sometimes the heat would be 125 to 130 degrees.

My mother was adamantly against smoking. My father would smoke an occasional cigar. I once asked my mother why we raised tobacco if it was so wrong to smoke it. I never did get a good answer. The same moral conundrum occurred in Moore County, next to the one in which I was raised (I was raised in Franklin County, TN). Moore County (Lynchburg) is the Jack Daniel's distillery home. It is legal to make Jack Daniel's whiskey in Moore County, but it is illegal to drink it. I never understood that one, either.

I had a relative who worked at the distillery who never, to my knowledge, drank alcohol. When I was a little boy, I remember hearing him remark that whiskey could be used as medicine for a cough. Seemed like a lot of cough medicine to me.

A few years ago, more so than now, some women were adamantly opposed to abortion but also used the intrauterine device (IUD) for contraception.

In some cases, the IUD allows conception to occur but does not allow implantation. Some anti-abortion women were constantly aborting. I never understood that, either.

Another thing I do not understand is why so many people are pro-life while many children are parentless. If one is adamant about protecting the unborn, why not be adamant about protecting the already-born? Sadly, many, many children will grow up in orphanages.

One could argue that it is not their place to raise these unwanted children; it is the parents' duty. I wholeheartedly agree, but the emphasis is on "unwanted." Their parents did not want them. One should deal with reality; these children are already here and would like a "pro-life."

I am told by many that I must believe the Bible literally. But then, when I read Paul's writings in Galatians 4:21-27, he writes that the epic about the two sons of Abraham was "an allegory" (Galatians 4:24, KJV or "taken figuratively.," NIV). Allegories are expressions using symbolic fictional figures. Thus, Paul is writing that not everything should be taken literally!

So, what does my "not understanding" mean?

We prefer to believe what we prefer to be true (to quote Bacon). I think we believe what we want to believe in, supporting what we already believe—selective perception and selective recall to use the proper names.

And maybe that is okay. Every year tobacco and Jack Daniel's continue to claim many lives and harm the lives of many other innocents. Some pro-life women still use IUDs, and many unwanted children languish their lives away in orphanages. I am fifty-six years old and still do not understand. Do you?

But then, maybe Jesus did. Maybe that is what He meant in Matthew 7:3 when he said, "Why do you look at the speck of sawdust in your brother's eye and pay no attention to the plank in your own eye." (NIV)

Better to Have an Inexact Answer

Article #90
The News Courier

John Tukey, the statistician, once wrote, "It is better to have an inexact answer to the right question than an exact answer to the wrong question."

This quote deserves a second reading to understand its depth. In my opinion, our social problems keep reoccurring because we keep giving exact answers to the wrong questions.

If I ask, "How do we help the poor?" The easiest answer is, "Give them money." It is an exact answer, but is it the wrong question?

This year is the fiftieth anniversary of President Lyndon Johnson's "War on Poverty." For fifty years, the government has offered many social programs to reduce the number of poor. But were the measures effective? We have reduced the number of poor among the elderly due primarily to Medicaid and Medicare, while the number of children living in poverty has increased. Overall, the number of poor has not been reduced.

What if in 1964, instead of asking, "How do we help the poor?" the question had been, "How do we help the poor to help themselves?" The answer to this question is difficult; it is inexact, but it is a response to a better question. It takes more time and effort to teach someone how to fish than to give them fish.

When I was a young man working my way through college, I worked at the farmer's co-op as a laborer making minimum wage, which was $1.60 an hour. I sacked corn, loaded and unloaded feed, drove trucks, and whatever else was needed.

One day I went to the grocery store and bought the cheapest food I could—bologna. I had driven there in my old car, which needed a paint job and tires.

When I went to pay for my bologna, I was in line behind a man wearing a 10-gallon hat, a leather jacket, and boots. He was buying a steak. I thought, *Someday.* Then he paid with food stamps. As I paid for my bologna with my earnings from my $1.60-an-hour job, I watched him drive away in a Cadillac. I worked for my tuna; he had been given his caviar.

Do not misunderstand me; I am not against helping people. I struggle with the idea of helping people who do not help themselves. If you eat enough bologna, you develop a desire to earn enough to buy a steak.

The ten-gallon hat, leather coat, and Cadillac man had been asked, "How can we help you?" rather than "How can we help you to help yourself?" The answer to the latter is inexact and challenging, but it is the more appropriate question, in my opinion.

Research by Thomas Stanley and William Danko has shown that the more parents give their children, the more children expect to receive. Children become less independent and less able to stand on their own feet the more they are given. They become less responsible.

The American family is a small-scale version of American society. Are we teaching America's "children" (the citizens) to be dependent on the "parent" (the government)? Are we teaching people to expect a steak when all they have earned is enough to buy bologna?

The answer to how best to help people is neither easy nor exact. But John Tukey was right; it is better to have an inexact answer to the right question than an exact one to the wrong question.

Truth Fragments: Driving and Getting Married
Part 1 of 3

Article #91
The News Courier, March 9, 2019

The "full truth" is an elusive concept these days. People who should know better seem determined to tell others they know the "full truth" and dictate our beliefs accordingly. Versions of the "truth surround us." The truth, according to the Democrats, is different from the Republican's version of the truth. The truth, according to Catholics, differs from the truth of the Protestants, which is somewhat different from the truth of Eastern Orthodox Christians. The list could go on and on. Truth takes many forms and is shared from many perspectives. Who are we to believe? What are we to believe? What do we cast aside?

This column cannot explain how we are misled by myriad "truths" that are not actually true. Instead, I discuss one methodology by which we are deceived. It is referred to as "not dropping the other shoe." This phrase has always mystified me. I have tried to find the genesis and trace the phrase's evolution with no luck. The connection between shoes and truth escapes me. So I coined a new term for my Critical Thinking class— "truth fragment." "Truth fragment," in my opinion, includes "not dropping the other shoe." It consists of both intentional and unintentional deception.

In either case, I want to emphasize that the person relating a truth fragment is not lying; they are just not conveying the full truth.

Most intended "truth fragments" come from politicians, lawyers, salespeople, medicinal advertisements, product advertisements, and others.

When a person relates something that they think is true but which is only partially true, they are sharing a truth fragment. What they say can be misleading. This person, however, does not know they are not "dropping the other shoe." They don't know they are leaving out part of the truth.

For example, we often hear that 90 percent of motor accidents occur within ten miles of home. The opposite is the real truth. This "truth fragment" may be unintended, but it is misleading. If I believe the truth fragment, I conclude that we become crazy drivers closer to home. The missing fragment is that 95 percent of all driving is within ten miles of home. Therefore, we become safer drivers closer to home. Think about it. If 95 percent of all driving takes place within ten miles of home, 95 percent of all accidents should occur within ten miles. Yet only 90 percent of accidents happen near home. Thus, the closer to home, the safer the driving. This example illustrates a "two-fragment truth."

Another example of a "two-fragment truth" appeared in a national newspaper. An article related that if a single man is looking for a wife, he should go to Sarasota, Florida. The city had more single women per man than any city in America. The same article said if a single woman was looking for a husband, she should go to Killen-Temple, Texas, which had more single men per woman than most cities.

When these were related in the news, they were true, but they were "truth fragments." Yes, Sarasota, Florida, had the most single females, but the second fragment of truth was that many of them were over ninety years old! Maybe they were widows who did not want to remarry.

As for the ratio of men to women in Killen-Temple, Texas, the second fragment of truth was that there is a huge men's prison in Killen-Temple. These men may want wives, but the weddings would be behind prison bars. Sort of puts a damper on the honeymoon, wouldn't you think? I do not think these deceptions were intentional, but "truth fragments" can lead us astray.

The "true truth" is elusive. Do your homework before your drive to Sarasota, Florida, or Killen-Temple, Texas. If you go, remember that when you get within ten miles of these cities, all the hometown people are driving safer than they do elsewhere. I will share two more examples in the next "truth fragment" article involving numbers 1, 4, and 5 and television stations.

Truth Fragments: Numbers and Television

Part 2 of 3

Article # 92
The News Courier, March 16, 2019

In Part 1 of this series, I explained how numbers could be used to deceive us. Today's "truth fragments" examples involve televisions and the numbers 1, 4, and 5.

The Number 1

The first example of "truth fragments" is repeated on local television stations. You probably have witnessed it if you are in an area with competing television stations. This example has three truth fragments.

Imagine this. One day, while listening to Station A during a commercial break, they claim their station "is number one in the listening area." The next day Station B claims they are number one and in the same area. Perhaps you wonder, "How could that be?" One must be fibbing. Then, low and behold, on the third day, Station C claims to be number one.

Surely you would wonder which station is telling the truth. Well, they are all telling the truth, but none are telling the whole truth. Here is what they are doing.

None of the stations is lying. Station A may have the number one show (first truth fragment) only on Monday (second truth fragment) and only at 6:00 p.m. (third truth fragment). Station B may have the most viewers, only at noon and only on Wednesday. Station C may be ranked first, but only at 8:00 p.m. and on Thursday. Sometimes when such claims are made, all three fragments flash briefly at the bottom of the screen in tiny print. No one could read the print because of its size and because it is gone before you know it.

Numbers 4 and 5

This second example of a "truth fragment" uses the numbers four and five and involves dentists and doctors.

Toothpaste and medicinal advertisements often claim that "four out of five dentists recommend *White Fang* toothpaste" or "four out of five doctors recommend *No Pain in the Behind* hemorrhoid medicine." These statements are misleading. One assumes they interviewed many, say 100 professionals, and eighty preferred the advertised product, say, White Fang toothpaste.

I'll use *White Fang* toothpaste to explain the deception in both cases. The deception is caused by small sampling techniques. The toothpaste company may have interviewed 100 dentists, but they divide the 100 by five to get twenty small samples of five dentists each. Within the twenty samples, say in sample 1, only 2 of 5 dentists prefer *White Fang*. The company does not use that sample for advertising. In sample 2, only one dentist prefers *White Fang*, so the company does not use this one either. Sample three has only 3 of 5 doctors who prefer *White Fang*. That's good, but it is not good enough. The sampling continues. By the twelfth sample of five dentists, 4 of 5 choose *White Fang*. This is the sample the company uses for advertising. Samples 13 through 16 are nothing to brag about either, but in sample 17, 4 of the five dentists again prefer *White Fang*. This seventeenth sample becomes the "and again in a *second* study 4 of 5 dentists prefer our toothpaste." Samples 18 through 20 prefer the other brand.

I illustrate this deception in my statistics class by having the students flip a coin five times and count the heads (*White Fang*) and tails (another brand). There is almost always one student who gets four heads and one tail and one who gets one head and four tails. Most students get combinations of three heads and two tails or two heads and three tails. This is the "law of averages."

Sometimes a student may get five heads and no tails. Have you ever heard "Five out of five doctors recommend" anything? I believe "5 out of 5" is too good to believe!

So, in this example, "4 out of 5" is the "truth fragment" you hear. You're not told that that resulted in only one or two samples out of twenty.

Some companies may count all one hundred dentists as a whole. I cannot claim that all companies have a "small sample." I can say that if the results do not support their product, you will never hear about it!

In part 3 of "truth fragments," we will analyze church burnings and breast cancer in women.

Truth Fragments: Church Burnings and Female Breast Cancer
Part 3 of 3

Article #93
The News Courier, April 20, 2019

Church Burnings

There was a brief period in American history, approximately eighteen months, in which thirty black churches were burned. Most of these fires occurred in the South. This was true, and many cited racial hatred as the motive. However, that was only one fragment of the truth. The fragment that was not well known was that twenty-nine white churches were burned in the same period. Thus, one could argue the motive was religious and not racial hatred.

I want to expand my comments on these church burnings because the incidents illustrate how numbers can be twisted to mislead. As a statistician, I know how to make church fires support racial or religious hatred.

One can believe that since fifty-nine churches burned, religious hatred was the motive. If I wrote that a black church was over four and one-half times more likely to be burned than a white church, one might conclude the burnings were racially motivated.

How can one claim that a black church is "almost five times more likely to be burned than a white church"? Here's how. During these eighteen months, there were approximately 350,000 places of worship in America, but only 65,000 were African American. That leaves 285,000 white churches. Thirty black churches divided by 65,000 is 0.0004615, and twenty-nine white churches divided by 285,000 is 0.0001017. If I divide 0.0004615 by 0.0001017, I get 4.54. Thus, a black church was over four and one-half times more likely to be burned.

In none of these statements have I lied. I dealt with all numbers as reported. However, I can give you single truth fragments or "twist" the numbers and influence your beliefs either way. Beware of truth fragments and twisting numbers!

Female Breast Cancer

Another example of a truth fragment would be the statement, "One in eight women, or 12 percent, in the United States, will develop breast cancer." The truth fragment left out is, "if all these women are over 80." Women who read this column should study an article entitled "Risk of Developing Breast Cancer" at www.breastcancer.org. This excellent article includes the missing truth fragment that most people omit and offers the most current information (December 20, 2018) I could find. The article relates the *average* chances of a woman developing invasive breast cancer for the following age groups:

- If you are in your twenties, one chance in 1,732=.06 percent.
- If you are in your 30s, one chance in 228 =.44 percent.
- If you are in your 40s, one chance in 69 = 1.45 percent.
- If you are in your 50s, one chance in 43 = 2.31 percent.
- If you are in your 60s, one chance in 29 = 3.49 percent.
- If you are in your 70s, one chance in 26 = 3.84 percent.

Now, if one adds the percentages in the right column, the total is 11.59 percent, or if rounded, 12 percent. Therefore, 12 percent, or one chance in 8, is the average *absolute risk* of developing breast cancer over an eighty-year lifespan.

Notice I italicized "absolute risk." "Risk" in medicine and other predictive fields has two different meanings. There is "absolute risk" and "relative risk." Absolute risk is the *average* probability of all women developing a certain disease, but *your* likelihood may be less or more than the average due to genes, race, ethnic status, and so forth. Relative risk means your chances of getting a disease are related to how you live your life. Relative risk percentages are found when comparing group A's risk to group B's risk of getting a particular disease. For example, women who imbibe two or more alcoholic drinks daily (Group A) have a higher relative risk of breast cancer than those who abstain from alcohol (Group B).

This column and the previous two have dealt with six examples of missing truth fragments in everyday conversations. These truth fragments can mislead us on topics including driving, marrying, watching television, buying toothpaste and medicine, burning churches, and developing breast cancer. All the examples involved numbers. Beware of truth fragments. Just think!

Foundations of Easter

Part 1 of 3

Article #94
The News Courier, April 6, 2019

Today I write as a student of early Christianity. By eighteen, I had read the entire New Testament and since have been intensely interested in the history of the early church. The Christian church has not always celebrated Easter; when it has been observed in the past, it has not been celebrated by all Christians. Furthermore, when it has been observed in the past, it has not always been celebrated by Christians on the same day.

The same is true today; not all Christians observe Easter. To the best of my knowledge, Christians today who do not observe Easter are Jehovah's Witnesses, Quakers, Hebrew Christians, and possibly some Presbyterian churches that follow the tenets of the Puritans. The Puritans of the past were strongly against it.

Of those Christians who do celebrate Easter, they do not observe it on the same day. This article and the next two address the question of celebrating Easter on different days, a certain letter about Easter, and what Christians read because of that letter.

Furthermore, I will discuss two dates, one that occurred in AD 325, which affects Christians one day each year, and the second that happened in AD 367. The second date affects Christians every day. Yet, I don't think most Christians are aware of these dates.

I have acquired from the Astronomical Society of South Australia 600 Easter dates that most Christians have observed from AD 1700 or will observe until AD 2299. Of the 600 Easters, most Christians will observe Easter only three times on March 22, and those three times were and will be years 1761, 1818, and 2285. For Christians, March 22 is the earliest, and April 25 is the latest when Easter can occur. The latest date, April 25, occurs only six times. Those six were and will be 1734, 1886, 1943, 2038, 2190, and 2258.

Passover

Easter is also called "Pascha" by some Christians; the term is connected to Passover, and what we now call Easter and its connection to Passover was of the utmost importance to the very early church. Passover is a Jewish festival beginning on the fourteenth (some sources say the fifteenth) day of Nisan, the first Jewish month of the year. It is followed by a week of using unleavened bread: The Feast of Unleavened Bread. That is the easy part.

The difficult part was ascertaining exactly when the fourteenth day of Nisan occurred. The Jewish calendar is a moon calendar. Over two weeks, the moon waxes (grows) until it is completely full and then starts to wane (becomes smaller) until it is invisible. Accordingly, it is a new month when the moon has been invisible for two days, and the thin crescent appears. But "who" ensured a thin crescent moon appeared in the sky? What if the nights were cloudy? For a more in-depth analysis, I refer you to an online article entitled "The Jewish Month" at www.chabad.org.

The time for this to occur is close to 29.5 days. To be exact, it is 29.5306 days. That half day causes problems. Because of that half day, there are two months with twenty-nine days in one year and thirty days in another. These two months are Cheshvan and Kislev.

The twelve-month lunar calendar is about eleven days shorter than a solar year, and a thirteen-month lunar calendar would be about nineteen days longer than a solar year. Moreover, this lunar calendar causes approximately 12.4 lunar months every solar year. Some Jewish years are twelve months, and some are thirteen months. The thirteenth month (leap year) is called Adar I.

So in a twelve-month lunar calendar, Nisan occurs earlier, and in a thirteen-month calendar, it happens later. Therefore, Nisan will be eleven days earlier each year for two or three years, and then the thirteenth month is added, and Nisan moves forward thirty days to correct the situation. (For further study, see the article "Judaism 101: Jewish Calendar" by Tracey R. Rian at www.jewfaq.org) You may ask why non-Jewish people don't have this problem. Well, most of the world has a civil calendar where the "moonths" do not follow the moon calendar. Thus we have months of twenty-eight, thirty, or thirty-one days!

Therefore, because of such problems, Passover can occur throughout the week, not only on Sunday. Around AD 120, however, Christian churches began voicing their displeasure with it not being on Sunday.

I do not think the movement that Jesus started, which was called the "Way" (Acts 9:1, 2; Acts 24: 14, 22 NIV), had a problem with it after his death. (Remember, his followers were first called "Christians" in Antioch several years after his crucifixion Acts 11:26 NIV). Jesus's brother James (Mathew 13:55, Mark 6:3, Luke 24: 10, and Galatians 1:19) was the head of this "Way" church (Acts 12:17; 21:18 and Acts 2:9, 12), and he was a zealous Jew (he would later be called the First Bishop of Jerusalem). I think James would have kept the fourteenth (or fifteenth) Nisan date, regardless of which day of the week it occurred.

The Term Easter

The term Easter may have originated with the word *Eastre,* a Teutonic (Germanic) goddess of spring, or from *Eastur,* which was a Teutonic festival of spring. Some people believe however, the term *Eastre* is descended from Astarte, the mother goddess of ancient Assyria, also known as Ishtar (Source: World Book Encyclopedia).

In Teutonic times, *Eastur* was probably a pagan festival celebrating Earth's resurrection and rebirth at the occurrence of the spring equinox. The early church, on occasion, adopted pagan festivals into its calendar because when pagans converted to Christianity, they did not want to forgo their festivals. The date for Easter is connected to the *moon and the sun* and not centered on the moon like Passover. This brings us to the importance of AD 325 when an important meeting occurred in the early church. We will address that in Part 2.

Foundations of Easter

Article #95
The News Courier, April 13, 2019

In my last article, I explained how Passover and its moving date became a problem for early Christianity because it was not always celebrated on Sunday. The issue became more prominent as time progressed during the first three centuries. At a meeting in AD 325, the date of Easter was determined. However, something else was considered first at the meeting.

AD 325

In AD 325, the first Nicene Council of the Christian church was held, so named because it was held in Nicaea in what is now northwest Turkey.

This council is recognized as the first *Ecumenical* council, which means the leaders of the *entire Christian world* were invited.

Emperor Constantine called this council to settle a large dispute in the church concerning the Arian views of the Holy Trinity. Around AD 318, Arius, a priest of Alexandria, Egypt, did not believe that the Father, the Son, and the Holy Ghost were equal. The Arian view was that God was above the Holy Son and Holy Ghost. There were believers on both sides. Arius lost the dispute, and the Nicene Creed was adopted; it is still recited today, but the original creed has been changed. After this decision, the Arian view existed in some areas of the Christian world for many years and exists today in the Unitarian Church, but it is not called the "Arian view."

At the AD 325 meeting, a fixed date for Easter was set. This decision occurred because of the growing uncertainty about when Easter should be. The uncertainty was centered around Easter and Passover and has been discussed above. Some Christian churches celebrated Easter on the first Sunday after the Jewish Passover, whereas other churches celebrated Easter at the same time as Passover and not Sunday.

The Council decided that Easter would be on a Sunday and that it would be on the first Sunday following the first full moon that occurs after the vernal (spring) equinox, which is March 21 of the civil calendar (Equinox "equal night"). On this date, there are twelve hours of sun and twelve hours of night.

Therefore, for Catholics and Protestants, the earliest date for Easter is March 22, and the latest is April 25. In this century, the earliest date was March 23, 2008; the latest will be April 28, 2038 (source: Astronomical Society of South Australia).

But not for Greek Orthodox Christians. Their Easter can be between April 4 and May 8 (www.thoughtco.com). There are over 800,000 Eastern Orthodox Christians in the United States (Source: Atlas of American Orthodox Christian Churches, 2011). Different sources estimate the number between 200 and 260 million worldwide. It has more numbers than any other religion in many countries of the Eastern Hemisphere.

Orthodox Christians

The Orthodox Christians, sometimes called Eastern Orthodox, have churches in America. They are the most prominent church in Russia, Eastern Europe, Greece, and western Asia. Eastern Orthodox beliefs are centered on the Bible but also on a *holy tradition*. The holy tradition consists of doctrines from the early centuries of Christianity. It can be said that Orthodox Christians value early Christianity customs more than Catholics and Protestants. Dating Easter is one of them.

As I have written above, the Nicene Council in AD 325 set the rules for the date of Easter (the first Sunday after the first full moon after the spring equinox). I did not include the last rule; its authority is a point of argument between Catholics and Protestants versus Orthodox Christians.

The debated rule is that Easter must occur after the Jewish Passover, which aligns with the biblical progression of events during Christ's Passion. Jesus ate the Passover meal before his crucifixion and resurrection (see Mark 14:12 and Luke 22:1). Therefore, if the Nicene Council ruled Easter must come after the Jewish Passover, most Eastern Orthodox Christians' celebrations of the resurrection can be seven to thirty-five days after the Catholic and Protestant celebrations. Thus, Orthodox Christians value holy traditions.

Catholics and Protestants don't follow this Passover rule because the church hierarchy and the theologians claim it is unnecessary and was not the intention of the AD 325 Council.

Fr. Jon Magoulias, a Greek Orthodox priest, disputes this, claiming the Catholics' and Protestants' refusal of the Passover requirement "is hard to understand since, by rejecting this provision of the council, they ignore the fact that the celebration of Jesus's Resurrection was celebrated at the same time from AD 325 to AD 1582, as well as the written witness of early church historians and even earlier canons...." For a more in-depth analysis, I refer you to this article by Fr. Jon Magoulias. It is entitled "Why Orthodox Christian Easter Is Later than the Catholic One" and can be found at https://usa.greekreporter.com.

Notice that in the year AD 1582, Western and Eastern branches went separate ways on the Easter date. Why? Because in 1582, Pope Gregory XII ruled that the Gregorian calendar would replace the Julian calendar. The Julian calendar was installed in 46 BC. The Julian calendar year was eleven minutes and fourteen seconds longer than the solar year. By 1580 it was incorrect by ten days. In 1582, Pope Gregory took ten days away from October to reset the calendar.

To make a long story short, Catholics, Protestants, and most of the world adopted the Gregorian calendar, but the Orthodox Church did not; they kept the Julian calendar! This became problematic, so in 1923, an inter-Orthodox Congress was held in Constantinople. It was decided to adopt a fundamentally similar calendar to the Gregorian one. Thus the dates for the holidays of the three main branches of Christianity were the same except for Easter; the Orthodox Church kept the Julian calendar! Thus the Resurrection celebration dates in the same year can be different by several days or weeks.

In conclusion, for the second column, I have explained the significance of the year AD 325 and how it has and will continue to affect Christianity. As for AD 367 and its importance for Christianity, a certain bishop living in Egypt sent a letter telling churches when Easter Sunday was to be held. But he added other instructions to his letter, which would become crucial for Christianity. I will address that in Part 3.

Foundations of Easter
Part 3 of 3

Article #96
The News Courier, April 20, 2019

I concluded the second part of this trilogy by referring to a very important letter written by a bishop living in Egypt. It was written in AD 367 and has affected Christianity ever since. Let us begin.

AD 367

Athanasius, who had been present at the first Ecumenical Council in AD 325, was a major opponent of Arianism, as described in Part 2. Because of his opposition to Arianism (remember, Arianism opposed the concept of the Holy Trinity), he was banished five times during his forty-five years as Bishop of Alexandria.

You may ask why Athanasius would be banished for his opposition to Arianism since Arianism "lost out" in Nicea in AD 325, as explained in Part 2. Good question. In reality, Arianism would remain strong in Egypt in the fourth century and continue until the 7th century in certain parts of the Christian world.

Athanasius first became the Bishop of Alexandria, Egypt, in AD 328. As discussed in Part 1 of this trilogy, the date for Easter changed every year. Therefore the Bishop of Alexandria would write letters every year to his brother bishops relating the date for Easter for that particular year. These letters were known as festal (feast) letters, and Athanasius would write forty-five of these during his role as Bishop of Alexandria from AD 328 until AD 373. On January 7, AD 367, he wrote his thirty-ninth of the forty-five festal letters relating the day for Easter to be celebrated. But he added something else; he listed the books that should be considered canon (scripture) for the Old and New Testaments. And very importantly, his list for the New Testament is the first that reflects the New Testament of today (Source and for more in-depth study: www.gci.org, the article is entitled "Church History: Athanasius lists the New Testament Writings").

You may ask, "Why the need for a list of the books for the Bible?" There were different opinions on what should be considered canon (scriptural).

Scripture: What Should Be Included?

Why the different opinions? Let me explain. I have a book in my study that contains many ancient scriptures that did not become canon (that is, these manuscripts did not make it into the Bible). The book is over 700 pages and contains the Gnostic Gospels, the Dead Sea Scrolls, the Visionary Wisdom Texts, the Christian Apocrypha, the Jewish Pseudepigrapha, and the Kabbalah (Source: The Other Bible, Edited with Introductions by Willis Barnstone, Harper One, 2005).

Due to the brevity of this column, I cannot come close to listing all of them. As for those "Old Testament" writings, there are many Psalms, The Odes of Solomon, The Martyrdom of Isaiah, and other Jewish writings. As for "New Testament" offerings, the list of the "Gospels" alone numbers 14. This list includes The Gospel of the Hebrews, The Gospel of Thomas, The Secret Gospel of Mark, The Gospel of Nicodemus, The Gospel of Bartholomew, The Gospel of the Ebionites, The Infancy Gospel of James, The Infancy Gospel of Thomas, A Latin Infancy Gospel: The Birth of Jesus and five other Gospels. I have read all of these, and they are very interesting.

As for other "Acts" that did not become canon, there are The Acts of John, The Acts of Peter, The Acts of Paul, The Acts of Andrew, and The Acts of Thomas. Again, very interesting reading if you are a student of early Christianity.

This book contains over 80 manuscripts that did not get into the Bible that most Christians use. There are even more ancient manuscripts not included in the Bible. Different Christian groups use Bibles that list other books.

Athanasius' List for the Old Testament

I searched for a copy of the thirty-ninth festal letter of Athanasius from AD 367 and found one at the Christian Classics Ethereal Library (www.ccel.org). The following is his pronouncement of what books should be in the Old Testament translated into English:

> There are, then, of the Old Testament, twenty-two books in number; for, as I have heard, it is handed down that this is the number of letters among the Hebrews; their respective order and names are as follows. The first is Genesis, then Exodus, next Leviticus, after that Numbers, and then Deuteronomy. Following these, there is Joshua, the son of Nun, then Judges,

then Ruth. And again, after these four books of Kings, the first and second being reckoned as one book, and so likewise the third and fourth as one book. And again, the first and second of the Chronicles are reckoned as one book. Again Ezra, the first and second are also one book. After these, there is the book of Psalms, then the Proverbs, next Ecclesiastes, and the Song of Songs. Job follows, then the Prophets, the twelve being reckoned as one book.
Then Isaiah, one book, then Jeremiah with Baruch, Lamentations, and the epistle, one book; afterward, Ezekiel and Daniel, each one book. Thus far constitutes the Old Testament.

So, were Athanasius' instructions followed completely and uniformly in "their respective order?" They were not. Check the order if you read a Protestant, Catholic, or Orthodox Bible. For instance, according to Athanasius, Job should follow the Song of Songs (Solomon), Daniel should be last, and other discrepancies exist.

Also, of the three branches of Christianity—the Catholics, the Protestants, and the Greek Orthodox—none have the same books in their respective Old Testaments.

The Catholic Old Testament contains the following books: Tobit, Judith, 1 Maccabees, 2 Maccabees, Wisdom, Sirach, Baruch, and the following additions to the Book of Daniel: The Prayer of Azaria and The Song of the Three Jews; Susanna; and Bel and the Dragon.

The Canon of the Greek Orthodox has all of the additional books of the Catholic Old Testament and adds five more. Those five are 1 Esdras, 2 Esdras, Prayer of Manasseh, Psalm 151, and 3 Maccabees. Moreover, 3 Maccabees is in an appendix to the Orthodox Greek Bible.

The Old Testament of the Protestant Bible has none of the additions of the Catholic Bible or Orthodox Bible. It does not contain Baruch as prescribed by Athanasius (Source: New Revised Standard Version of the Harper Collins Study Bible including Apocryphal Deuterocanonical Books, Student Edition, General Editor, Harold W. Attridge, Harper One, 1989).

Athanasius' List for the New Testament

The following is Athanasius' proclamation for the New Testament translated into English:

Again, it is not tedious to speak of the [books] of the New Testament. These are the four Gospels, according to Matthew, Mark, Luke, and John. Afterward, the Acts of the Apostles and Epistles (called Catholic), seven, viz. of James, one; of Peter, two; of John, three; after these, one of Jude. In addition, there are fourteen Epistles of Paul written in this order. The first, to the Romans; then two to the Corinthians; after these, to the Galatians; next, to the Ephesians; then to the Philippians; then to the Colossians; after these, two to the Thessalonians, and that to the Hebrews; and again, two to Timothy; one to Titus; and last, that to Philemon. And besides, the Revelation of John.

So, were Athanasius' instructions for the New Testament followed? Not immediately. For decades, there were differences of opinion about which books should be in the New Testament. The books that became canon and were most controversial were: Hebrews, James, Jude, 2 Peter, 2 John, 3 John, and Revelation. Those that created strong convictions that did not make it into the Bible were Shepherd of Hermas, Epistle of Barnabas, The Acts of Paul, and Apocalypse of Peter, among others (Source: Funk and Wagnalls, New Standard Bible Dictionary, 3rd edition).

The Greek Orthodox Church would break away from the Catholic Church in the Great East–West Schism of AD 1054. The Protestant movement would begin in Europe in AD 1517. Owing to the beginning influence of Athanasius' letter, all three branches today have identical New Testaments. For those of you who are students of early Christianity, however, you will notice that the books do not follow the order of Athanasius.

About the Author

Mark W. Durm, PhD, is a Professor Emeritus at Athens State University in Athens, Alabama. He spent thirty-eight of his forty-seven years in higher education at Athens State University. His primary areas of instruction were critical thinking, statistics, and physiological psychology. Durm has more than fifty professional publications and authored approximately 100 newspaper columns. His research has been quoted in books, peer-reviewed journals, magazines, and national newspapers, including the *New York Times* and the *Washington Post*. His research, coauthored with Jane Sweat, focused on the  use of psychics by police departments and was the subject of a Japanese television documentary. Durm has received inquiries about and requests for copies of his research from at least fifteen countries and many universities in the United States.

Durm, a Desert Storm veteran, served in the Tennessee Army National Guard, primarily at the Tennessee Military Academy and the 300th Mobile Army Surgical Hospital.

Durm owns and heads a company that invests in real estate in Alabama and other states. He has three children who are the joys of his life—Spencer, Sydni, and Sophia. He resides on his farm in Athens and continues to research and write.

www.ingramcontent.com/pod-product-compliance
Lightning Source LLC
Chambersburg PA
CBHW061151120626
46546CB00005B/2010